A
FAMILY
BLESSED

Dan Rotthoff

TEACH Services, Inc.
P U B L I S H I N G
www.TEACHServices.com • (800) 367-1844

Copyright © 2019 Dan Rotthoff
Copyright © 2019 TEACH Services, Inc.
ISBN-13: 978-1-4796-0902-4 (Paperback)
ISBN-13: 978-1-4796-0905-5 (ePub)
Library of Congress Control Number: 2019934211

All Bible texts are taken from the King James Version (KJV). Public domain.

Published by

TEACH Services, Inc.
P U B L I S H I N G
www.TEACHServices.com • (800) 367-1844

Reviews

"Truly led by the Holy Spirit."

—*A. Balkins, Jr. MD*

"Some people have the capability of packing a whole lot of adventure in their lifetime. Even for a man like Dan Rotthoff who is reaching close to 100 years the suspense and intrigue has never subsided. If you seek true life adventure you will love how God helps Dan dodge death and disaster from being stranded in the mountains in the dead of winter to crash landing in Alaska in a small aircraft he was piloting. In between these events he helped make a youth ranch possible. In short you won't and cannot put this book down once you start."

—*Tom Sanford, Founder of Project Patch*

"It was only as I became older that I realized just how blessed I was as a child growing up-to be raised by loving parents that not only provided a life of fun and adventures but the guidance and example to live a life of faith in our Savior. THANK YOU, Dad, for writing this book! It will long be a family treasure—for generations to come."

—*Dawn Carter, Daughter*

"Dan Rotthoff has had a most interesting life—from being a Pennsylvania farm boy to a paratrooper in the US Army to service as a Christian pastor. His biography spans nine decades of unique experiences and takes the reader from adventure to adventure in clear, concise prose written from the heart as well as a keen memory. Many descriptive words still fall short of capturing the essence of this man—cowboy, pilot, minister of the Gospel, philanthropist, businessman, outfitter, guide, salesman. Yet the reader will appreciate his humility, modesty, and love of God and family. This is a fascinating story told by a fascinating and truthful man."

—*Don Lojek, Attorney and Pilot*

"It's impossible to capture a lifetime in a book. What's clear in reading Dan Rotthoff's story is that his life has made an impact. This is a story of determination, hard work, and flexibility. Dan isn't afraid of hard work or adapting his strategy as new opportunities appeared. It's hard to describe Dan. Most men are identified by what they did for work and he's done a lot of different things, including working as a farmer, trapper, sawmill owner, Army Airborne paratrooper, salesman, business owner, rancher, outfitter, and missionary. You could describe him for his adventures, of which he had many. He also is a devoted son, husband, father, and patriarch of the family. But what stands out to me is that he is a man of character that others trust and is faithful in the tasks he is given. I've known Dan for many years and am thankful for him writing this book that allowed me to appreciate him and our God even more."

—Chuck Hagele, Project Patch Executive Director

"Whether you are needing spiritual encouragement for yourself or for a loved one, this book provides guidance and heartfelt words to help you on your journey. My husband and I both enjoyed the author's sincerity and personal experiences shared, and we can't wait to recommend the read to others."

—Judy Jarnes, Retired Administrative Assistant and Sabbath School Leader,
and Rolf Jarnes, Educator, Youth Leader, Church Elder, and CRNA

"Cowboy, lay pastor, and author Dan Rotthoff is a good friend of mine, and I am honored to share a paragraph about his new book, *A Family Blessed*. I was blessed and enriched as I read the manuscript. His pen bleeds with ethos as he looks back at the adventurous nine decades of his life and spills his treasure trove of memories onto the pages of his life story. He does a masterful job of telling his story that spans the spectrum from the predictable to the unpredictable, the serious to the humorous, and the sad to the joyful. A major theme he carefully weaves throughout his family history is God's providential leading and watch care of Rotthoff and his family. He gives the credit and glory to God for all the positive and good that he experiences in life. He concludes the book by extending a genuine and heart-felt appeal to the reader to know Jesus as Lord and Savior, and to experience the joys of salvation. *A Family Blessed* is interesting, inspirational, and engaging. You must spend time between the covers of this memoir!"

—David Prest Jr., President, Idaho Conference of Seventh-day Adventists, Inc.

"Prepare for an adventure with the author as we travel down the tracks of his life, through the eyes of human interest and a detailed history of a time long past. Rotthoff takes us along for a ride through decades of interesting details and reflections of a humble and grateful spirit—a man's life well lived. While his life is full of tragedy and gut-wrenching moments that impact a man for life, there is also a hope and joy that runs alongside these fascinating narratives. Throughout it is apparent that his faith carries him along, overcoming great struggles, while maintaining an outlook that good would always somehow come from what life would bring his way. His great love for his wife, Margie, and their family is evident at each turn of the road. Their odyssey literally crosses the country through different jobs, opportunities, and life challenges. You'll enjoy this journey with Dan, as you prepare to be entertained, inspired, fascinated, and encouraged."

—Fred Cornforth, CEO of CDI Group of Companies, Author, Former Pastor

"Dan Rotthoff is quite a story teller. His journey through life makes a great read, and is rich in much-needed old fashioned values and practical spiritual lessons for each one of us today. His love for his family shines out clearly. Being a family man myself, I can really relate to his desire that all of his relatives to discover God's incredible love and wonderful plan for their lives. I pray that *A Family Blessed* will warm, enrich, enlighten, and bless many hearts."

—Steve Wohlberg, Speaker/Director, White Horse Media

Table of Contents

Preface

The original intent of this project was to invite all of my family into a closer togetherness. It was to be directed to my children, my grandchildren, my great-grandchildren, and to all their families. It is my hope and prayer that this drawing together will result in everyone then becoming part of the everlasting family of God.

Should there be others who have occasion to read these stories, I hope that their hearts will be touched so that someday soon we can all have the promised blessings of fellowship together in that eternal home that is even now being prepared for us by our loving God.

—The Author.
Ritter, Oregon, 12/20/2018.

NOTE: All numbers in parenthesis refer to numbered pictures at the back of the book.

Introduction

I enjoy a good read, but I treasure a compelling life story.

My friend Dan has chronicled an autobiography of a life journey of fourscore and ten years that is at least fascinating. But I think you will find that, as you finish this journey of a life of service, you also will be inspired.

I first met Dan a few years ago, when he showed up in Alaska with a strange request.

"My wife passed away recently, and I still have a few good years to serve my Lord. I want to be a missionary in the Arctic."

I was astonished, and I must admit, more than a little skeptical as to the value of an octogenarian in the harsh Arctic climate. But I soon learned that age was irrelevant with this senior. He was a man with drive, experience, wisdom, and a passionate love for his God. We placed him in Togiak, Alaska, on the Bering Sea, and there he became a wonderful shepherd to the Eskimo people. That was the rocky start of a deep friendship that has fed the inner springs of my soul.

I can only sum up his story, in the words of a wonderful old song:

The Lord's our Rock; in Him we hide,
A shelter in the time of storm;
Secure whatever ill betide,
A shelter in the time of storm.
Mighty Rock in a weary land,
Cooling shade on the burning sand,
Faithful guide for the pilgrim band—
A shelter in the time of storm.

"Those who bring sunshine into the lives of others, can't keep it from themselves" (James M. Barrie)

You will be richly blessed by the journey through an ordinary life of an extraordinary child of God.

—Kenneth C. Crawford,
Alaska Conference President (Retired)

A LONG TIME AGO

A Little Family History

A long time ago, in the twentieth century, in the 1920s, I was born in my parents' home on Virginia Street in Aspinwall, (16) Pennsylvania. Virginia Street was located in a section of a suburb of Pittsburgh, on what was generally known as "The Hill in Aspinwall." I was the second child, having a brother something over a year older than I. He was named after our father, Walter. (9) Neither of them ever had a middle name. Nor was my brother to be identified as a junior, but throughout his youth was known as Bud or Buddy. (2, 78) The handle my parents fastened on me was R. Daniel, and I forever after answered to the call of Dan. And so begins my tale.

Of course, all I know of my parents' courtship is what I have been told, simply because I was not there at the time. My father had been a brakeman on the railroad as a young man when he decided to join the army. Since he was too young to join without his parents' permission, he assumed his older brother's name (Adam) and age, then joined on his own. He joined the cavalry. He was in for less than a year. I don't know how the military found out, but I have a copy of his Honorable Discharge, which records the fact that his age when he joined was sixteen years and ten months. He was discharged from the army in November of 1919. He was later discharged from the National Guard in September of 1920. I do not have a record that would show if he was a member of the National Guard when he joined the army or if that was a later enlistment. His enlistment in the army was during the First World War.

After his discharge from the army, he took a job as a mechanic at the Ford dealership where he worked for many years. He lived at home with his parents, who were trying hard to find a good Christian girl for him to go with. It seems that Anna, Adam's young wife, knew a young lady by the name of Margaret, (5) who was a member of the German Seventh-day Adventist

Church and had invited her to Mom and Pop's home. Father came home from work and headed upstairs to his room when he noticed the girl sitting in the living room. He went upstairs, cleaned up, then began the courtship.

My parents, Walter and Sarah Margaret, as a young married couple were building the home (16) I was born in. I believe it to have been under construction when Bud was born. I was the only one in the family to have been born at home.

They sold the home when I was perhaps four years old and began a moving odyssey that continued until I was sixteen years old, at which time Father was tragically killed. I will provide the details to this event later in my story. For now, I will attempt to be as accurate as possible in providing information on our parents and grandparents, where they came from, and what part they played in our lives.

My father was the youngest child of twelve born into the family of Fredrick and Mary Jane Rotthoff. (1) They were known affectionately to all the grandchildren as Pop and Mom Rotthoff. Pop was born in Germany and immigrated to America as an eighteen-year-old. He came from Germany to build the first blast furnace in the US. He did not go back to Germany. I do recall that he had successfully learned the English language almost to perfection, which was unlike so many who spoke with a broken use of their adopted tongue. It is my understanding that he worked in the steel industry which was the industry that Pittsburgh was most remembered for during the nineteenth and most of the twentieth century. I remember him as a kind and friendly person, with a ready smile.

Mom was the only one of my parents and grandparents who was born in the United States. Her birthplace was in Washington, DC. However, her father's side was German; her maiden name was Mary Jane Crux. My knowledge of her family history is without substance. I remember her as a good homemaker, her home was always clean and attractive, and the outside of the home at 109 Delafield Ave. in Aspinwall was neat and presentable.

As a young lad, we attended church at the Pittsburgh First Church, and our family always occupied the front pew. I remember that Pop would sometimes attend church with us there on the first pew, always with a good nature. I have memories of that front pew, having to sit quietly during the service, dressed in itchy woolen "knickers." Knickers were the mode of dress for young boys at that time. For those of you who may not know what knickers were, they were boys' pants that came to the knee or just below. Mom was having some health issues, so I do not remember her going to church with us.

Coincidentally, Pop died in 1937 at the age of seventy-six years and one month and Mom passed away in 1939 at the age of seventy-six years and ten months.

They had twelve children, of which my father was the youngest. As I became a part of the family, there were only seven of the twelve still alive. Some had died as small children, no doubt from children's diseases, which was very common during the nineteenth century. Unfortunately, I don't have those records. The seven that I remember as a child were two of my father's brothers: Adam, who was about three years older than Father, died in 1972 at the age of 73, and Fred, who was perhaps as much as ten years older. He died, I believe, in the 1960s. I do not have any record of his death nor do I have the records of the deaths of his sisters. I do, however, have some fond memories of both uncles and all four aunts.

The aunts were: Emma Hildenbrand, who lived in New Jersey; Lenora Bierman, who lived in Pittsburgh; Gus Stark also lived in Pittsburgh, and Gert Shannon lived in Aspinwall. Aunt Emma had at least one son, but I never met him. Aunt Lenora had one daughter, Mary Jane, who I remember was with her mother when I stopped in to visit while on my way to be inducted into the army. When I left, she walked with me and gave me a hug as I boarded a streetcar and headed for army duty. She, of course, was quite a bit older than I. Aunt Gus and her husband John had two sons, both of whom were killed in a motorcycle accident before I was born. Aunt Gert and her husband Jack had one daughter, Jean, who died when I was very young, of leukemia, I believe.

Mother's maiden name was Sarah Margaret Vollberg. (5, 45) Her parents were Wilhelm (which I understand to be William in English, and so he became known) Vollberg and Anna Schmidt Vollberg. (18, 29) They were Grandpa and Grandma to me, though I never really knew him. He was born in Germany, and she was born in Austria. I don't know much about their coming to America. I know they were married in Pittsburgh. Both had been married before. He had three sons Wilhelm (William), Heinrich (Harry), and George, and one daughter Marie Rosalie. These were half brothers and sister to my mother. Grandma had one daughter from her first marriage, Anna. I met the three boys, but not Grandpa's daughter.

With regards to Grandma's daughter Anna, her family and ours maintained a very close relationship for many years. She and her husband, Uncle Bay, had two sons, Paul and Lewis, who were several years older than Bud and I. Both have been dead for a number of years at this writing. Lewis had no children. Paul had two sons and a daughter. The daughter works in the Vatican in Rome, and the two sons live in Carnegie, Pennsylvania. The oldest, Paul Jr., maintains a very close connection with our family. He has been deaf all of his life but has overcome this handicap in almost every way. He reads lips, understands sign language, has a college education, earns a good living, and travels all over the world, besides being a real gentleman. I believe he is a couple of years older than our son, Dan.

My mother has one full sibling, a brother, Carl, who was two years younger than she. Carl was a high school teacher in Pittsburgh. He and his wife Bertha moved to Florida sometime around 1960, I think. Their son, Carlton, became a medical doctor and is now retired and living in Tennessee. His son, whom I have never meet, also named Carlton, lives in Tennessee, too, is a medical doctor, and has three grown children. Wow!! Time slips away. Sometimes I think that perhaps I have had an experience something like "Rip Van Winkle." Probably, most that read this will wonder who he was.

Years ago while I was perhaps seven or eight years old, I asked my grandma Vollberg why she was so short. In her distinctive broken German dialect, she responded, "Daniel," (she always called me Daniel) "ven you get oldt, you grow like the horse's tail."

My Early Years

Having provided a brief outline of the history of my grandparents, uncles, aunts, and cousins, I will now relate more current information on my generation. As mentioned above, my family moved from the home on Virginia Street in Aspinwall, where I was born, then moved again, then again. Let me see how many homes I remember living in. There was an apartment on Brushton Ave., an apartment on Race and Starrett Streets, a home on Bennett Street, Oh, yes, there was a home we rented; I believe it was on Babcock Blvd., in Millvale, a suburb of Pittsburgh.

While there I took the initiative to become a door-to-door salesman. I sold *Life and Health* magazines. I think the price was ten cents, and I had to pay a nickel for each one. The money I earned helped pay for some of my own clothes. Then we moved to a country home in Fox Chapel, but a big move was next to a

One day on our way home while crossing a street, I was hit by a car.

twenty-acre farm in Butler County near Saxonburg, then to a fifty-eight-acre farm a few miles away, then to Dorseyville, back closer to Pittsburgh, and finally to a 180-acre farm 135 miles north to Erie County, and one mile north of Wattsburg.

I don't remember if the first move was to the Brushton apartment or not, but I do remember that we lived on Bennett Street when I started school. Bud and I would walk to and from school. One day on our way home while crossing a street, I was hit by a car. Though I have no recollection at all, I was taken to the hospital, whether by auto or ambulance, I don't know. Bud ran home and told Mother that I was hit by a car, but he didn't know how serious the accident was, but he did know that I wet my pants. I spent several days in the hospital, then in bed at home. The bedfast period at home lasted a long time, because I first came down with chicken pox, and then when I was just recovering, I came down with the mumps. I recall getting out of bed and being taken out the front door, where I was shown the sign that warned the public of these communicable diseases. The law required for the home to be quarantined for both chicken pox and the mumps at that time.

The apartment we lived in on Race and Starrett street was over a little store that was owned by an elderly Italian man. I still remember his description of the bottles of pop that he sold. "Vat you vant? Orangeapopacherrysoda." It seemed to me that everything he sold cost either a penny or a nickel. Directly across the street was the Pittsburgh Church, and in its basement was the church school I attended. I think I was in the second grade, and my teacher was Mrs. Robinson. When I did something naughty she would say, "Now Danny, lay out your fat little patties on the desk," and she would give them a few paddles with a ruler. Can't figure out why she called them "fat," because I

> *Teddy wandered behind Uncle's car as he started to back out and was run over.*

wasn't fat, maybe just big. We played "Kick the Can" for recess. Played right in the street. Between the sidewalk and the curb there was a little dirt and that was where we played marbles.

Then there was the move to Fox Chapel. Our parents were determined to raise their children in the country, out of the city. Our home sat alone on a country road, though some distance up the road there lived a family by the name of Stallsmith. This family had five young, beautiful daughters. Directly across the road from us, was the County Prison Work Farm. It was a pasture for their dairy cattle.

By this time Bud and I had a baby brother. His name was Theodore John. (10, 18) A little curly, redheaded adorable addition to the family nicknamed Teddy. Teddy was walking, but was still an infant, when one day Mother's brother, our uncle Carl and his wife Bertha, was visiting us. Teddy wandered behind Uncle's car as he started to back out and was run over. At least we were informed that the car had actually passed over his body, though I find it hard to believe, since after we rushed him to the hospital and spent some days there, he came home and survived, seemingly without complications.

Sometime along the way, our father and mother found a way to purchase a very nice twenty-acre farm in Butler County. This was in the mid-1930s. Bud and I attended a one-room country school at Hannastown, about two miles from our home across the fields. I was in the fourth grade. By now, at last, my parents wish for a baby girl was realized. Wow, and another wow. She was named Lenora Jane (11, 18) and the whole family took on a new attitude. Now the family was complete and would remain so.

It was a difficult time for our mother, though. Pop Rotthoff had passed away the year before, and Mom Rotthoff was having some serious health issues. It was necessary that she be moved into our home, and the responsibility of her care fell to our mother. This, along with managing three growing boys and a new baby girl. I remember that the stress she experienced was very evident. Mom Rotthoff passed away in our home there on the first farm.

Father worked as a mechanic at Humes Brothers Ford dealership in Aspinwall, about thirty miles away. I believe this dealership was the oldest, or at least among the oldest in the nation. He worked there for many years and was considered a valued employee. Mr. Hume gave each employee a ticket for a new car. My father was the lucky one and won the vehicle. It was a brand-new Studebaker. The roads in the Depression were not anything like they are today. Even so, Mother and Father were determined to raise their family away from the cities.

We had one cow, a calf, and some chickens. Of course, Bud and I had been raised away from livestock and had no knowledge of reproduction. I remember one Sunday Dad led the milk cow a couple of miles to a neighbor by the name of Earl McGill, who had a bull, and we two boys went along to keep the cow moving.

The farm was too small, so they sold it and bought another one about three miles away. It had more than fifty acres, several cows, several goats, a team of horses, and lots of chickens. The farm was purchased lock, stock, and barrel, which also included several pigs. Of course, the pigs were sold immediately.

The house had no indoor plumbing. The outhouse was a couple of hundred feet away over near the barn. It was a fairly large facility, with three sizes of holes, one to fit every posterior. On the back of the building, was a lift-up door, and inside it was a sled where the team could be hitched to it, and its contents carried away to be scattered on distant fields. As long as we lived there, it fell my responsibility to take care of that chore. No one else would get involved.

Father had a ready market for the farm produce with his fellow workers. Almost every day he would take eggs, dressed chickens, cows' milk and cream, and even some goats' milk. So it contributed to the stability of our finances, which was very important during those difficult Depression years. Mother did most of the milking twice a day, although I remember that Bud and I would once in a while exercise our hands in the milking process. Mother had purchased a large cream separator and would put the milk and cream in containers as per the orders received. I remember when we lived in the city that raw milk was delivered on the front porch in glass quart bottles. So our operation fit right into what was the mode of the day. I remember the cream rising to the top of the bottles. Homogenized milk was yet unknown. Of course, we always used cream on our rolled oats in the home and on the homemade fruit pies that were a pretty regular part of our diet. The skim milk was fed to the chickens.

It was always my responsibility to chop the heads off the chickens and help with removing the feathers. Mother did all the dressing and packaging of the dead birds. In spite of these activities, everyone in the home were vegetarians. I believe that Father and Mother became vegetarians when they were married and raised all four of their children as such. I never tasted meat until after my father died, and I went on the road at seventeen years old as a truck driver for Mayflower Transit Company all over the United States. Bud and Janie (I always referred to my sister by her middle name, although the rest of the family have always called her Lenora) to my knowledge, never tasted meat throughout their entire lives.

I remember one year I raised a number of turkeys. Father got orders for them, and though I was a fair-sized pre-teen, I remember the struggle I had in convincing those big birds to let me take their heads off.

I believe the year was 1939 that I became involved in the "profession" of fur trapping. There was a little stream near our home, and I received some tutoring from a neighbor on trapping muskrats. After obtaining some #0 steel traps and donning my rubber knee boots, I set out on what became known as a trapline. Of course, I had to run the trapline before going to school. Lo and behold, I had two muskrats. Since I had been given the fundamentals of skinning, I was a busy entrepreneur. All this, plus doing my regular chores. Then walking close to three miles to school. After moving to this farm, I went to the Jefferson Center School. If there was not much snow, I could cut across country and reduce the distance about a mile. Furs during those years of the Depression were worth a lot of money. Muskrats were worth from $1.60 to $2.00, and that was a lot of money. Skunks were worth up to six or seven dollars if they were mostly black, at least three dollars with a volume of white on them. Beavers were worth a fortune, but there were none near the farm. A weasel was valued at 25–60 cents. I did not have the expertise to trap the fox.

Let me tell you about the first skunk I caught. I had asked my parents to let me buy a .22 rifle, but the answer was a firm NO. It happened to be a Sunday morning when I caught this smelly fellow. So I got a short piece of galvanized pipe and fearlessly brought it to bear, but before it made contact, I was shot full in the face with a load that blinded my eyes and knocked me to the ground. After a little while, I was able to find my way back home. I was met by my mother who immediately commanded me to disrobe there in front of the house. She then buried my clothes in the garden and dragged outside the large wash tub that we took baths in. She heated some water and had me scrub with enough vigor to remove skin. She later said that when she kissed me good night for more than a month, she could still whiff the memory of the skunk. But I still had to kill the skunk. It was necessary for me to walk two miles to a neighbor whose kids also trapped. They had a .22 and walked back with me and shot it. It could have taken considerably less time, but no one in the area had any phones.

But I then got permission to purchase a gun of my own. It seems that the single shot .22 cost me six dollars. I had that gun for many years. Trapping turned out to be a big help and continued to develop some lasting memories. It was necessary to ship through the mail to sell the furs. I remember the name of one company I shipped to was Hawbakers Trading Post. One time I took a package of furs into the post office and the postmaster said, "Danny, you will have to take this back home and do a better job of wrapping it." Which I did. The money I made was mine, and my parents allowed me to do with it as I wished. I bought my own clothes, and I purchased a new "two-wheeler." That made my journey to school much better. It was at that time that brother Teddy started in first grade in the Jefferson Center School, and I learned to ride him on the crossbars of the bike.

Bud and I were the farmers. We learned to harness the horses by one of us taking the hames and the other the breeching; we would then put two milk stools in beside the horses, and by standing on the stools, we could get the harness on. We plowed an eight-acre field, one driving the team, the other holding the walking plow upright, then it only took one of us when dragging or harrowing. A neighbor came and harvested the grain with a McCormick binder, which we then hauled into the barn. Then in the fall, the threshing machine came, and the grain was separated. The corn was harvested with a corn knife and put in shocks with the use of a special wooden sawhorse. Then when it was good and dry, and winter came, the family would get together on the large barn floor, and with the use of a husking knife, husk the corn. So many memories. So much nostalgia.

The War Years

I remember on a snowy evening, December 7, 1941, Father came home from work. When I saw him pull in, as usual, I went out to meet him. He gave me a tight hug and said the Japanese had bombed our possession in Hawaii, and we would be at war. I was just in my thirteenth year, so was really not old enough for the impact to sink in deeply. But I do remember we had one of those large floor model RCA radios, and though there was considerable static, we all hunkered down close to it and listened as President Franklin D. Roosevelt reported to the nation that we had declared war.

Changes began to happen. I think it was along in the spring or early summer many things were rationed, gasoline being one of them. That created problems for my father getting to work. The result was that the farm was sold, and we moved to Dorseyville, perhaps less than ten miles for his commute. We rented the second floor of a farmhouse owned by an elderly couple. I could still trap, or so I thought. I had to walk through some large fields to a stream, but after a little while, I determined that there were no muskrats there. There was a line of mailboxes, and I wondered how many of those mailboxes my .22 would shoot through. I know I found out, but I am unable to remember how many of the mail boxes I could actually shoot through. A few days later, a deputy sheriff came to the house and talked with Mother. I was reprimanded, but no spanking, and they did not take my gun away from me. That is when I found out that crime does not pay.

There was a family of black folks that lived across one of the large fields. Their name was Short. They had a son my age, and we became very good friends. His name was Henry Short. We spent a good bit of time together. One day I was visiting at his home, and his father was going to butcher a pig. He asked me if I would shoot it for him. Sure, and I did. That turned out to be my first successful big game hunt.

For a couple of years, while we were living at the farm in Butler County, Bud traveled with our father every day and went to church school in the city, while I kept going to the one-room country school and took Teddy with me. But after moving to Dorseyville, I traveled to the church school also. We would go to work with Father, then take a streetcar and make a couple of changes to get to East Liberty where the school was. Then reverse the procedure and get back to Aspinwall. Soon I would take a different streetcar through Etna, to the end of the line, then hitchhike home.

Unbeknown, at least to me, Father was taking some classes on aircraft engines. When he had finished the course, he obtained several letter recommendations (including one from Humes Brothers, his employer) directed to the General Electric Company, in Erie, Pennsylvania, where they manufactured aircraft engines for the war effort. The result was that he was offered a job, so once again we were on the move. They purchased a 180-acre farm just north of Wattsburg, which was about twenty miles from Erie. The farm had a large three-story home with about fifteen rooms in it, two large barns and a well that produced mineral water, which had been sold to the public in the past. The year was 1943, December, I believe. The world was deeply involved in war.

Brother Bud was away attending school at Mount Vernon Academy, in Mt Vernon, Ohio, a Seventh-day Adventist boarding school. I should note at this time that Bud was and always had been the scholar of the family. Learning always came to me with difficulty, not so with Bud. He was always an "A" student, while I always struggled hard to achieve a "C" grade. Besides, I disliked school and always considered it a waste of time. My mind always drifting off to more worthwhile projects like skinning a skunk or hitching the team to the sled under the outhouse. Not that I necessarily enjoyed some of these duties, but they were a reality of life. I did attend the local Wattsburg High School, grudgingly.

Summer did finally make it, and Bud was home from Mount Vernon. We worked together on the farm. We had some dairy cows and milked them all by hand. Mother, of course, was involved, and we shipped milk to the milk co-op. That fall I remember after Bud returned to school in Ohio,

I found a bee tree. It was a large sycamore in the pasture between the barn and French Creek. A neighbor, George Hoag, who had experience in harvesting honey from bee trees, came one night with some kerosene lanterns, a two-man cross-cut saw, an axe, a wedge, and a sledgehammer we went to work.

This turned out to be a big job, taking most of the night. We felled the tree, then moved to where the hive was and cut into it with the saw, cutting about halfway through the trunk every twelve or fifteen inches. Then we took the wedge and split those sections out. The trunk was hollow for a considerable distance, and in that cavity, was a wealth of the sweetest honey you ever did see or taste. We had brought with us the milk buckets but had to go back to the house and get a large wash tub. It was no doubt the same one in which a few years earlier, on a different farm, I had tried in vain to remove the odor from a certain skunk. (Now, of course, we did have indoor plumbing and no longer needed a wash tub for taking the family baths). The net result of that venture was four milk buckets and one large wash tub filled with honey. Laboriously, we packed it all back to the house, where for a couple of weeks Mother labored in draining the honey from the combs. She put a bed sheet into a bucket full of honey, hung it in a warm closet, put a bucket under it, and it would drip, drip, and drip. Then she placed it in quart jars. What an experience.

The farm was on both sides of the highway. On the east side were the barns, the well house, the pasture, French Creek, and the bee tree. On the west side were the house, garage, and the farmland. The large Wattsburg Fairgrounds (considered to be the county fair) was enclosed on three sides by our farm. On the east side was our pasture and French Creek, on the North, were the barns and on the west was the highway and all along the highway was our farmland. The fair was always on Labor Day Weekend. It drew large crowds of people from Erie and all over the county. There was never near enough parking within the fairgrounds, so we would always have a crew to organize parking on our property. It seems like we charged twenty-five cents per car. It made for some extra income.

Tragedy Strikes

This brings me to the most dramatic moment to have ever affected the family, at least up to that point—the sudden and unexpected death of our father. It was Labor Day afternoon, the first Monday in September 1944. It was a national holiday, but because of the war effort, Father was working at the General Electric plant in Erie building aircraft engines. During the afternoon a violent thunderstorm went through the area causing a great deal of damage. On the front lawn of our home were several very large hard maple trees. A limb on one with a diameter of fifteen or eighteen inches, was blown out of the tree across the highway, and lodged in the high-tension lines. The power company had been notified and had turned the power off. The fair was shutting down early because of the damage and the loss of power. The highway was overloaded with bumper-to-bumper traffic.

I had brought the cows in and had done the milking. It was somewhere between six and seven o'clock. I had built an electric fence around some of the meadowland across the highway from the barn, the crops had already been harvested, and the grass had grown up providing some good pasture for the cows. So they had to be moved across the highway. Father had come home from work and was at the house. I went over and asked him to come and stop the traffic while I took the cows across the highway. There was a roadway between the barns and the well house. I was walking behind the cattle as they went up that roadway and across the highway. When I came out to the highway, I looked to the right and saw Father lying on the ground beside the highway. I was overwhelmed to see some wires on the ground that were "dancing" around him and making sparks that I could hear.

A neighbor, Roy Huntly, who dealt in cattle, stopped, and he suggested that we get a garden tool with a dry wood handle. So we ran to the garage, and we took a hoe and a garden rake. We were successful in pulling the hot wires away from Father. Roy and I carried Father across the highway and laid him on the lawn in front of the house. By then, quite a few people were gathered around. I rolled Father over and was trying to administer artificial respiration, but they pulled me off.

The school nurse was there and said, "Your father is already dead."

It was later determined that he had been killed instantly. It was a telephone line, charged with the high-tension current that circled him. I seem to remember that the current in the high-tension line had been increased to 72,000 volts (I believe that was the number that was stated) to supply the extra current required for the fair. There was an electrical burn on his forehead and another on one hand.

Most of the rest of that day is pretty much of a blur. I do remember going back to the barn and shoveling some manure around.

George Hoag came in and tried to encourage me some. I remember he made the statement that "time is the great healer-up." Though it did not make much sense to me at the time, it is a fact that God uses time in this manner to aid us in the continuance of life.

Over the years I have often considered how without warning Father's life was taken from him, just standing there waiting for me to call out to him that the cattle were on their way up to the highway and to stop the traffic. No premonition on his part that the end of life was imminent, nor was there any premonition on the part of any member of the family. Often, I have thought of life and death. How unsure it is. I think of how important it is for us to be prepared. It is my prayer that every member of my family, myself included, come to realize and understand how suddenly and quickly life can end. Sometimes, without any warning. Are you prepared for such an eventuality? Am I?

Bud came home from Mt Vernon. Mother suffered terribly, but she was a strong woman, and with the help and direction of God, she was able to keep the family together and lived until she was eighty-four years old. Father was laid out in our home, and the funeral was under the direction of Pastor Eric Beavon, pastor of the Erie and Corry Seventh-day Adventist churches.

After things settled down somewhat, Bud went back to Mt. Vernon to finish his education. Teddy was old enough to understand, at least in part, how the tragedy affected the family. He was in grade school in the little two-room country school in Lowville, less than a mile from the farm. Janie, of course, was a preschooler, and I am sure that it in itself was an important factor with Mother, having her at home and the companionship that she offered. I never returned to school again, having been projected into an entirely different lifestyle.

It was determined that a power company employee threw a switch in a sub-station that reenergized the line when my Father passed under it. Times were different then than now. Mother tried to see if legal action could be taken, but for some reason, she accepted the counsel of someone to settle. If I remember correctly, she settled for $750. I believe that Bud's academy tuition was taken care of by our Aunt Lenora, an older sister of our father. But it was a fact that with two very young children and a mortgage on the farm, Mother faced some difficult financial times.

Allow me a little time and space to recognize and pay tribute to our loving and merciful heavenly Father who did indeed see our mother and the family through this experience. As her children, grandchildren, great-grandchildren, and great-great-grandchildren view this history of the family, I pray that you will visualize the many ways that God leads in our lives and that each of you will determine in your own heart to turn your life over to Him, and to do it now. There is a lot of danger connected with putting it off. Think of the circumstances that surrounded the death of my father. For my part, I choose to live each moment as if it were the last moment of my life. The rewards both in this life and the life to come far outrank all that this world has to offer.

Janie and I are all that is left of this family. Both Buddy (February 1, 2014) and Teddy (January 10, 1998) have passed away, and I am now an old man—a fact that was brought to me recently in a face-to-face meet-ing with a doctor. He told me that I was doing well; keep doing whatever it is that you are doing. I said if I am doing so well, why is it that I am so weak and always so tired. I didn't use to be that way. His response, while leaning across his desk and looking me in my eyes, "Mr. Rotthoff, you're an old man."

OH!! He was only confirming what I already knew. But seriously, some morning each of you will wake up and discover the same thing. And the reality of this comes much faster than you imagine. My father was only forty-four years old, so he was not privileged to have ever gotten old.

Making My Own Way

Most of my life from this point on, was lived away from my family. That meant that I had little contact with my siblings and with my mother, and hardly any contact with the extended family. The exception was, for a year or so after the death of our father, I took care of the farm. I did the milking and other chores, used the team to plow and harvest the fields. Then the next winter, Mother was having some difficulties, and I took on a new project. When they bought the farm, the sellers, Mr. and Mrs. Gilmore, held the mortgage. I don't remember what it amounted to, and the Gilmores were kind and good people. On the farm was a "sugar bush" that had not been tapped for a number of years. (Sugar bush is a timbered area with hard maple trees that are tapped in the early spring, and then the sap is collected in buckets and taken to a large boiling stove where it is boiled down to maple syrup).

With a two-man crosscut saw, working alone, I cut these large trees down, bucked them up into eight-, ten-, and twelve-foot logs, then took the team and skidded them to the highway. I found a man that would loan me a few hundred dollars to buy an old 1930-something Ford ton-and-a-half truck with log bunks on it. I got some skids, and with a peavey hook, I loaded the logs by myself. Then I took them to Corry, about twenty miles away, where there was a factory that made bowling pins. The only kind of wood they used was hard maple. I sold enough logs for Mother to pay off the mortgage. Here is a great deal of hard evidence that God was overseeing the affairs of this Rotthoff family. I look back at this and other experiences in my life with sincere amazement. There is no way that a dumb city kid, with very little qualifying aptitude, in his mid-teens, could have achieved this goal. It was because of the family's belief in Jesus Christ and God's direct blessings that made it become a reality.

Spring came to the year of 1945. I was intrigued with logs and the lumber industry. I already had a truck with log bunks on it. Someone told me about an old sawmill for sale over near Corry. Sure enough, there it was, and it was all complete. It swung a sixty-inch circular saw, had a three-bunk steel carriage, all of the husk was complete with the belts and pulleys. It had an old Buick auto engine for power. The wheels, axels, and the body had all been removed, leaving the motor, the frame, and the driveline. A pulley sheave was installed on the driveline. A flat six-inch-wide belt close to forty feet long traveled from the drive pulley with a six-inch-diameter to a forty-inch-diameter and ten-inch-wide pulley on the mill shaft. Interestingly, the large circular saw had a crack that started under an inserted tooth section about three inches toward the center of the saw where a ¼-inch hole had been drilled to stop its advancement. The man who had loaned me the money to buy the truck thought I was a good risk since it had been repaid, so he loaned me the several hundred dollars to buy the mill. Don't remember the amount, but I am sure it was less than $500.

An elderly neighbor and member of our church, Thaddeus Butler, who had some background in sawmills, agreed to help me get it set up and in operation. There was a man in Erie who hammered circular saws, giving them the correct tension to stand up and not wobble at a given rpm speed. Old Thad's expertise in getting the mill set correctly was a very technical job. The husk had to be set on a good foundation, the track that carried the carriage, that carried the log into the saw had to be super critical. The Buick engine took time to get it set so the belt would track accurately on the pulleys. The motor was set at an idle with a long cord fastened to an upright on the husk that I could pull for power and rpms as I fed the log into the saw. After some adjustments and building a deck for the logs at the level of the carriage, we were in business and cutting good dimension lumber. The tail-sawyer would pile it up; then when we would be shut down, we would put it all on stickers.

Nearly all the timber in that northwestern part of Pennsylvania was hardwood, and it was in demand by the furniture industry. There were a couple of good-sized factories in Union City, about nine miles from us. We cut hard and soft maple, beech, elm, some red oak, ash, and a few other species. It took some little time to learn how to saw for grade. No heart could show on the lumber, or it would reduce the grade and, of course, lower the value. The heart was usually made into pallets. Most of the demand was for 4/4 and 5/4, plus an eighth of an inch. Though I remember so well an order for a couple of railroad cars filled with 16/4 green elm. We hauled truckload after truckload to the rail siding at Union City and by hand carried them into boxcars. The dimensions were four inches thick and random widths and lengths. Some of these pieces weighed three to five hundred pounds. We had no mechanical equipment to aid, just our frail human backs and a strong determination. Don't remember what this lumber was to be used for, maybe building a bridge.

In delivering lumber to the furniture factories, I would place two layers of boards on the log bunks, then place a two-inch steel pipe across the width of the truck a little less than half the length of the lumber to be loaded. Then go ahead with the load. When loaded, the front of the load would be in contact with the two layers on the bed, and the back part of the load would be several inches above it. When directed to where it was to be unloaded, I would take the chains and binders off, back up and spike the break, and away it would go. Then, of course, the front of the truck was several feet off the ground. But I would have plenty of traction, and it would come down slow and easy if I moved very slowly forward. Then I'd unload the bottom tiers, retrieve the chains, binders, and the pipe, and be gone.

Bud graduated from Mount Vernon, I think, in 1945. He and his girlfriend Virginia (Sweetie) Krause were married April 6, 1947. Sweetie still lives there seventy years later is still affectionately known as Sweetie. God bless you, Sweetie. (15)

Bud decided to get involved with the farming, and since I was single, I took a job (at seventeen years old) driving a Mayflower Transit moving van all over the USA. I wonder what would happen if a trucking company would hire a seventeen-year-old now? I spent two or three weeks moving locally in Erie and learning how to pack furniture into the trailers. A couple of older fellows took me under their wings and taught me the trade. All the old road tractors were Reo and Federal trucks with sleepers on them. But when it came time for me to go on the road, they could only get me a brand-new White without a sleeper, and it had bucket seats. So the only place to sleep was in the trailer with some furniture pads if it wasn't loaded to the hilt.

New vehicles for private use had not been available since the war started, but moving companies had priority, because they moved a lot of military personal. So there I started on a new venture. I was paid $1.03 an hour. No overtime, but I could work as many hours as needed. We had to fill out a log, but I never once had to show it to anyone, so all drivers were working a week or two in the future. All the highways across America were two-lane, there were no limited-access highways, and the road conditions were not to be compared with what they are today. Oh, yes, I forgot the Pennsylvania Turnpike, a toll road had been built before the war, but that was only from Irwin to Carlyle. That was quite a highway. I never made it to the West Coast, but had some moves to Texas and the other Midwest areas. When loading or unloading, I would go to a local bar and try to hire a few guys to help. The company would wire me the cash to pay them.

Military Life

The next chapter in my life was as I turned eighteen and had to register for the draft. I was somewhat enamored with the prospect of parachuting out of an airplane, and rumor had it that they paid extra for your having the privilege of jumping out with a parachute. I found out that the 11th Airborne Division was to move into the occupation of Japan from their presences in the South Pacific. So I enlisted. Basic training was given at Fort Dix, New Jersey. Base pay for a buck private then, I believe, was thirty-two dollars a month. Then after I went through jump school and was awarded my wings, my pay would jump another fifty dollars a month. Then when I shipped overseas, I would qualify for an additional 20 percent, making a total of $98.40 a month, plus all my food, and all clothing, boots, and medical care. I did send an allotment to my mother, where they took something out of my pay and added a little to it and sent her a monthly check. (48)

After completing basic training at Fort Dix, I was given a "delay en route" so I could visit home before shipping overseas. I rode on a train with a steam engine to Erie, then on a new diesel-fired Pullman train all the way to Oakland, California. That was some memorable experience. I was served first-class meals in the dining car and had private quarters to live in. Wow! Some experience for a young country boy. Then I was taken up the Sacramento River to Camp Stoneman.

After a week or two of processing, I was loaded on a troop ship along with four thousand other young men and headed out under the Golden Gate Bridge into the wide Pacific Ocean. I believe that I was the only GI on the ship that was not seasick. The toilet facilities on a ship are called the head. It was necessary for me to step over the bodies of super sick young men when I would make my way to the head. I remember the regurgitated substance of their meals sloshed back and forth as the ship rolled from side to side. There were not many that showed up in the galley for meals those first few days. But I was always there.

Then the weather changed, the seas became smooth, and everyone recovered. Even so, I don't remember it as having been a pleasant South Pacific cruise. The sleeping accommodations were interesting. The bunks were piled four high with barely enough room to crawl in. The ceilings were low, so four bodies on bunks in a tier between floor and ceiling were rather tight.

After about three weeks, the ship docked in Guam for a couple of days. I remember standing at the rail and looking into the clearest water in the world and watching large sharks swimming and looking for some American GIs to nibble on. Then we sailed on to Yokosuka, Japan. As far as I know, I was the only 11th Airborne recruit on the ship. All the rest of the 4,000 on board were headed for other units. The 11th Airborne Division was headquartered at the northernmost part of the main Japanese Island of Honshu; the town was known as Yokosuka.

> *I was loaded on a troop ship along with four thousand other young men and headed out under the Golden Gate Bridge into the wide Pacific Ocean. I believe that I was the only GI on the ship that was not seasick.*

For a while, I was given the job of being a truck driver, later as motor-pool dispatcher, and then later as the company mail clerk. At that time, because there were still hostilities, no GI's were allowed off the base unless traveling in a convoy. To keep our jump pay, it was necessary to make a parachute jump every month, and, of course, training exercises were a regular part of military life. Some educational classes were offered, and I took one on typing, for which I have been eternally grateful. I also took a short course on the Japanese language and one on American history. The base did have a good library that I would frequent as time would allow.

Upon receiving an invitation to visit the Seventh-day Adventist mission in Tokyo, I took it into the commanding officer. I had a furlough coming, but I was greatly surprised when he said, "Sure, I will give you authority to go." So began my trip through the countryside of Japan without any other companions. But I never encountered any problems or difficulties, except to deal with the language barrier.

The missionaries were just returning to Japan. The church had recalled them when hostilities were becoming serious before the war. Most were returned to the United States, but Paul and Retha Eldridge and their two young children were sent to the Philippines. There was apparently no thought that Japan would invade that country. But as it turned out, that family spent the entire war years in a Japanese concentration camp. Retha Eldridge (89) wrote the book *Bombs and Blessings*. I treasure my copy of that book that she gave me.

The two weeks I spent with the missionaries there was a high point in my life. I stayed in the home of Francis Millard and his wife; he was president of the mission. B.P. Hoffman (90), an older gentleman who had spent many years in Japan and knew the language very well, took me under his wing We visited points and items of interest including a visit to one of the great shrines and images of Buddha. While I was there, the mission conducted the largest Christian meeting that had ever been held in Japan. I sat up in the balcony with Mrs. Millard who interpreted for me, with tears running down her cheeks, as best she could the message that was being delivered by Elder B.P. Hoffman. That very large auditorium was filled with every seat taken. It seemed that the war being over the people were hungry and willing to learn about Christianity.

Back to the base and military duty. Eventually, I took another long ship ride across the Pacific to Camp Stoneman, California, where I was discharged. On that ocean trip home, we did stop for a few days in Hawaii. I remember so well the many sunken ships in Pearl Harbor. Some lying on their sides, others in devastating positions partially out of the water. I will never forget that visual picture of the effects of war. We had the opportunity to spend a little time walking the streets of Honolulu. Quite a difference from my Pennsylvania background.

A Civilian Again

Then I went on to Camp Stoneman and back into civilian life. After discharge, a friend, whose home was in Spokane, Washington, and I were trying to get public transportation to our homes. This was still in the aircraft piston engine days, and since it seemed the whole world was trying to get home, no seats were available. We tried the bus station, and he was able to get through to Spokane, but no luck for me. It was a couple of hours before his bus was to leave, so I checked my luggage on his ticket, and we went to a restaurant. When we came back, we found that the luggage had all been sent on an earlier bus. I did still have a small suitcase, but my big duffle bag was on its way to Spokane. He promised to retrieve it and keep it for me until I got there.

The discharge gave us a nickel a mile (I think), or for me it amounted to about $150, to get home on. So I started out hitchhiking. In hitch-hiking over the mountains in northern Idaho, I passed through the most outstanding country in the world. I remember commenting to myself, "Someday, I'm coming back to live in this country." About twenty years later, sure enough, we were in Idaho. Not in that northern tier, but Garden Valley has a great deal in common with it. There can be no doubt that God had been leading in so many areas of my life, and this hitchhiking experience was one of them. There may be experiences in the lives of all my readers, that are not clear to you now, but let me assure you that God has a plan, and if you give Him a dominate place in your life, you will be amazed at the results.

Though it was around the first part of March, winter was in strong force in that mountain region of the mountain west and the upper plains states. That travel experience was one I shall never forget. Of course, this country had much different social concepts in the late 1940s as is evident today. Seldom did I find it necessary to stick out my thumb. When some-one would let me out of their car, many times another car would come along and stop while I was getting my duffle bag out of the back seat, or out of the back of a pickup truck. Some would go out of their way to get me to where they figured I would have a better chance to get a ride. I remember one lady who took me miles out of her way.

Every night I stayed in a hotel. Of course, there were no motels, but each town or village had a hotel or at least a boarding house. Hotel rooms were available for $1.50 to $2.50 a night. I ate all my meals in a restaurant, sometimes as a guest of my benefactors. I kept a record of all the expenses I incurred on that trip home of about three thousand miles. They totaled either twenty-three dollars and some cents, or twenty-seven dollars and some cents. Can't remember which.

Coming into Fargo, North Dakota, the temperature that day was forty degrees below zero, and I think the wind was blowing forty miles an hour. Maybe I was exaggerating a little, but not much. The cars and pickups had different heaters and defrosters in them, but for the most part they were fairly comfortable. For sure I never was standing alongside the road for any length of time. Always there was someone happy to give a ride and some interesting conversation.

It's Good to Be
Back Home Again

Home again, and so very good to see the family again. Mother seemed to be doing well, my little brother and sister had grown, and Bud and Sweetie were running the farm. I am not sure, but I believe that they were just getting the farm started in raising strawberries as opposed to milking cows. This turned out to be their vocation and avocation for the next fifty or sixty years. Bud became the national president of the strawberry association and developed many innovating growing procedures that have proven successful.

Having been up in an airplane dozens of times but never having the chance to land in one, I decided to buy an airplane and learn to fly. I bought an AERONCA Champion, (17,88) a two-seated, tandem airplane with a ninety-horse Lycoming engine. A step up from the Piper Cub. It was just two or three years old. These had been built during the war for military reconnaissance work. This plane cost me $300, and I paid an instructor three dollars an hour to teach me to fly. Eight hours of instruction and I had my solo license. I used a field on the farm and flew it everywhere I wanted to go. I would fly to Pittsburgh. The commercial airport there was Allegany County. The new Greater Pittsburgh airport was still some years in the future. Commercial aircraft were still all piston; jets had not yet been introduced. There was a tower, but my plane had no radio. So I would circle the tower and when permission to land was given, they would shoot a green light at me, and I would use the active runway.

Bud wanted to go for a ride with me, so we went up and flew around the countryside for a while so he could visualize it from the air. He became air-sick in the back seat, so we headed in for a landing. We were on the final approach, just seconds from touchdown. He pulled open the window on the left. As he came to the point of no longer being able to retain his lunch, he tried his best to throw up outside the widow, but his seat belt did not quit allow him to fully reach the opening. The only part of his regurgitation that went outside was a tooth that he had on a plate. But he was not discouraged, years later, after I had moved to California, he bought an airplane and even designated a strip on the farm and had it placed on the charts.

My old sawmill was still there under its cover, but at that time, feeling that God had blessed me in so many ways, I felt the desire to share my faith with others. So I decided to sell spiritual books door to door. The conference office for the church was at Pittsburgh, and that is where I headed. I bought an older LaSalle car for a few hundred dollars and lived in a boarding house in Aspinwall.

As summer rolled around, the West Pennsylvania Conference of Seventh-day Adventist was putting together their annual summer camp for children, and they asked if I would come and be one of their (6) counselors. (7) I don't remember the name of the place where it was held, but it was over closer to the central part of the state. Also present was a beautiful young lady who was a professional swimmer, and it was she who was in charge of the waterfront teaching the children to swim and learn about water safety. (6, 13) Her name was Margie, later to become known as Nana.

We became good friends, and as the camp came to a close, some of the management invited Dick Barron and the staff for a little social event. Dick Barron and his brother Henry had been the main speakers and spiritual leaders for the camp. Dick had been the song leader and associate of George Vandeman's at a recent series of evangelistic meeting in Pittsburgh. Dick and his wife and Margie and I became good friends that lasted until Dick's death many years later. Dick's life story is most inspirational, much of it recorded in the book *Comes the Whirlwind*.

Starting Married Life

Margie and I began courting and were married on March 12, 1950. (96, 97, 8) Home from our honeymoon, we moved into a duplex in Wattsburg and settled into a long and happy marriage, loaded with many challenges, many successes and a few failures. We immediately determined to own a farm, and after less than three months, with the help of the Farmers Home Administration, we purchased a dairy farm off Highway 89 a number of miles north of Wattsburg. (30)

A beautiful preteen young lady, Carolyn, (44, 32) was a part of our home from the very beginning and has remained a part of the family ever since. Because of her, Margie and I supported the establishment of the Lowville Church School (28) from which she graduated and then went on to Mount Vernon Academy in Ohio for her high school. Then as time went on, she married Arthur Longstreet from the Wattsburg area. (94, 67) I gave her away, as her father, at the wedding in the Erie Seventh-day Adventist church. Their family developed into three beautiful daughters, Karen, Sandy, and Rhonda. We all remain close as a family unit, though each of the girls has their homes and families now. (22, 23)

Following are some of Carolyn's memories of those early years:

"My dad and I had a really good visit at my home today. While we had lunch, we talked about the long-ago times and the many good times we had. This is my story of that time as I remember it; when Dad became my father.

"I was born March 9, 1937. Twelve years later my mom and I found ourselves a family of two. That summer, Mother went to a church camp to teach swimming. That was her job, and we loved it. I could swim from the time I was little and used to go with her and had a lot of fun. While she was at the camp, she met Dan.

"I remember Mother telling me about Dan; he had an airplane, how neat he was, and that he wanted to meet me. I remember being in Dan's life right to begin with. He took me up in his plane, and we did a stall. It made my tummy feel funny. A lot of stuff happened later in that summer and fall. I felt he cared about me; he took me to work with him in the evenings when mother was working.

"Mother and I went to live with friends of Mother's, the Padens. Dan would come and visit us there. He would drop notes tied to rocks from his plane for us to read. Sometime later Mother told me that she and Dan were going to get married. I remember asking if I could call him Dad. When they came back from their honeymoon, my present was a 45-rpm record with the song "Daddy's Little Girl." He has been Dad to me ever since.

"After a few months, we moved to a farm about seven or eight miles from the Rotthoff farm. I became Dad's boy. He called me Hank! I loved Dad so much; he became my world. I was loved and wanted, and he made me feel that way. I still have some things he gave me, his wings, his old army coat, and I wore that coat all the time. Mother said she couldn't get it off me.

"Well, life went along with new experiences I'd never dreamed of. I got my first calf named Binky and a goat. I worked in the fields with Dad. I would drive the team while he pitched hay on the wagon. I loved being Dad's boy, Hank.

"We had an old car that sometimes would not start. Our home was on the top of a hill sloping in every direction. One Sabbath morning Mother and I were all dressed ready for church. Dad coasted down the hill to get it started, then turned around to come back and get us. When he got to the top, he just kept right on going and waved as he went by. He turned around again and then got stopped for us. He was laughing and said the brakes didn't work when he came over the hill.

"The next year we were blessed with a baby boy. I remember when I first saw him in the hospital. He was crying, and two men were looking at him in the nursery. One of them said 'That's OK, kid, I'd cry too if I were the only boy in there with all those girls.' I said, 'That's my little brother.' I was fourteen years older than he when I went to Mount Vernon Academy. When I came home on break, he always wanted to sleep with me. I had him learn funny little sayings. When I started to go on dates, Danny went with me a lot.

"When Mother started me in the church school in the fifth grade, I was Carolyn Rotthoff. My marriage license and any documents where it asked for my maiden name have always been Rotthoff, even my girls' birth certificates. I am so happy. Thank You, Lord, for taking my life in Your hands. If it had not been for my father Dan, I don't know what would have happened to me.

"My little sister was born when I was 17. I love her so much. Mother would bring her to MVA where I was in school when she was five or six months old. I would show her off like she was a doll. When she learned to talk, she called me mama and Mother 'Mother.'

"Dawnie was fifteen months old when I got married. My brother was four and my Bible-bearing man. Dad walked me down the aisle. Before we started, I was so nervous I just kept hanging onto his arm. He said, 'Come on, Hank, we don't want to have to send all those presents back, do we?' That made me laugh, and the rest went great.

"Arthur and I started saving money in a Little Black Sambo bank for the birth of our baby. When the bill came, we were short, and Mother and Dad paid the bills. We were so happy we didn't have to leave her at the hospital.

"When Dad and Mother made the move to California, we wanted to go along. I think it took us six months to get things in order for us to follow them. Dad made arrangements for an engineering job for Art, and they had a house ready for us to move in.

"Ten years later Dad and Mother bought a big cattle ranch in Idaho. They built a beautiful home overlooking the river. We visited them Christmases and in the summer. Dad gave horses to Karen and Sandy. Then six years later, we followed them to Idaho. In addition to the cattle ranch operation, they had a youth guest ranch operation and a big game hunting business.

"Dad and Mother started a subdivision and Art fit right into that operation. In 1975 we made the move to Idaho. Karen wanted to finish her last year of high school in California before she came along. Sandy finished her last three years of high school at Gem State Academy. Rhonda started in fifth grade in the Garden Valley school.

"In 1997 Arthur was diagnosed with a brain tumor at the end of July and died in November. My brother Danny and sister Dawn have been a great part of our family's life. My whole family from Dad and Mother have had a very special bond 'one for all and all for one.' I am still here, finding things a little harder to do now, but with God's help. I hope for Jesus to come soon. I want to see you all there too."

February 4, 2018, Carolyn Longstreet.

Farmer Dan

Back to the move into the farming operation in Pennsylvania. A very good dairy barn and a good three-story house was a part of the purchase. There was no indoor plumbing in the home except for a hand pump in a small kitchen sink. It had a good wood-fired cookstove, upon which Margie canned a thousand quarts of fruits and vegetables each year. We purchased a new wood heating stove from Montgomery Ward. It was round, not more than two feet in diameter, and was fired from the top by lifting a door that was about half the area with the chimney exhausting from the balance of the top. That was years ago, and I have never seen another stove like it since. But it did a good job of heating the house. The second year we did acquire an electric cook stove, but Margie had fallen somewhat in love with the old wood-fired cookstove, so continued to use them both.

Also, that second year, we did install running water in the kitchen and put in a modern bath. The next year I made a deal for a new furnace and struggled to put it in the basement. That also made life better. Of course, country homes built for that era did not have adequate insulation, and windows were single paned. I remember in our bedroom, with a west-facing window, many nights during the winter enough snow would accumulate on the window sill and on the floor to make a couple of snowballs.

But the farming, the dairy, and the fieldwork occupied our main efforts. We also did all our fieldwork with horses for the first two years. (37, 100, 102) Did all the plowing with a walking plow, drilled in the oats, planted the corn for silage. Nana took the challenge to sit on the sulky cultivator. The first two years we milked by hand, then acquired a used Hinman vacuum milking machine.

Another year or two later we bought a new cultivator and drove the team to cultivate the corn. When harvest time came, we had two teams, and I would put together a three-horse hitch on the McCormick harvester. Then some weeks later the threshing machine would come with a crew of neighbors to separate the grain. What a wonderful life. Seriously, there are so many memories of great value. These were good years. No doubt I am guilty of boring some of my friends when I get into the mood to relive those experiences.

About the second year of our marriage, Nana and I had the desire to share our faith. So a plan was designed to put on a laymen's set of public meetings, and the location chosen was Titusville, a small city located about 30 miles south of Wattsburg. We named the meeting "A LAYMAN SPEAKS." After some searching, I found a public hall owned by the American Legion or Odd Fellows, or some other organization, and made arrangements. The town also had a radio station, and I arranged to be on the station for fifteen minutes one day a week. Bud and Sweetie and a lady from Lowville, a Mrs. Kuhn, would travel with us. The meetings were to only be on Sunday evenings. Sweetie would play the piano and provide special music. Sweetie has a very beautiful voice.

The radio program was to be recorded on a tape at home and taken to the station. The first program was fifteen minutes of complete silence, and no one on the radio indicated that it was to be anything other than complete silence. I canceled that part of our effort. We did have a pretty good turnout, and it seemed that everything went well. Much better than we expected.

The attendance seemed to increase the next Sunday night and we developed some interaction with some of the folks. About the third night, I related a quotation from Socrates to impress a point that I was focusing on. The correct pronunciation of that distinguished name is Soc-rea-tees. I pronounced, So-crates. The mistake did not bother me until we were driving home, and Mrs. Kuhn told me the correct pronunciation. Wow, at least I was successful in showing my ignorance. It was late on a winter evening, so it was dark, and the redness in my face did not show.

The happiest times of all we experienced as our children came into our lives. Carolyn, already a part of the family, claimed ownership of a dog, a calf, and a kid goat all at one time. Somewhere in the archives is a picture of her with them all. Then in the spring of 1951, we were expecting the birth of an entirely new person. Doctor Henderson was the young doctor who took care of Margie through that prenatal care period and the birth of our son Danny in the Stem Memorial Hospital in Union City. He also did the postnatal care for mother and child. He did all this for a standard fee of twenty-five dollars.

It was a mile from our home to Highway 89, and Carolyn had to walk to meet the public-school bus. She went to our church school in Lowville, but we were given permission for her to ride on the bus. She recently reminded me that she was complaining about having to walk that mile to and from the highway. She remembered me telling her that when I was her age that I had to walk four miles to school and four miles back home and all that distance was uphill both ways.

Nana was pregnant with Danny, and we were snowed in with no chance of the snowplow making it for a day or two. So rather than dump the fresh milk, I decided to hitch the team to a set of bobsleds I had and take it to the highway. Our phone was one of the old hand-cranked party line phones that hung on the wall. Our phone number was 17J, and that meant four long rings. Margie called the milk hauler and said the milk would be at the intersection. She wanted to ride with me. That was good, as it was a beautiful winter day, and a good day to be out. In turning around in the deep snow at the intersection the bobs tipped over and threw Nana out. Of course, I was concerned, but she was OK. She was tough.

As Margie came to term, and I would take her to the doctor, I no doubt registered considerable impatience. One time the doctor said to me, "You are just anxious to open a surprise package. Take Margie for a ride on a bumpy road; that may speed things up somewhat." So I did. We had an old 1935 Chevy sedan, and we bounced along at a pretty good clip. Rough roads were not hard to find then. But it did not help. The day did come finally, and we hurried into the hospital almost fifteen miles away. I had already convinced the doctor to permit me in the delivery room, something that was against policy of all the hospitals at that time. So I went in with Margie, and the head nurse proceeded to kick me out. I said no, I had permission to be there by the doctor. She would not hear of it. Finally, he came and said, "Let him alone, he is OK." That permission was still good three years later when another great event was taking place, the birth of daughter "Princess" Marleah Dawn. However, during that three-year period, the doctor raised his fee to fifty dollars. (34, 35, 19, 20, 21, 24, 25, 26, 27, 36, 50)

We didn't hire a lot of help, but there was always a need for some as the dairy herd grew in numbers. About the time of Danny's birth, we had a man working for us by the name of Charlie Lord. (31) Though he appeared older, I believe his age to be in his late fifties or early sixties. He was a pleasant fellow, but he had a rather unusual handicap. He had a very large hernia in his private parts, as large as his head and it bulged visibly in his pants, requiring him to wear pants several sizes larger. However, in spite of this, he was always working with a steady effort. I had sent him to cut corn in a field that I had leased. The field was just to the east of our farm and was within sight. It was fall, and the corn was ripe. He would cut it with a hand-held corn knife and put it in shucks. Presently, Margie saw him coming up the hill toward the house looking very strange. When he got close to her, he reached into his jacket and pulled out a beautiful rooster ring-necked pheasant. He said it flew out near him and he threw his corn knife and to his surprise, hit it and killed it. Of course, it was not hunting season, and his strange mood indicated his fear that a game warden would throw him in jail. He asked if Nana would cook it. She agreed if he would take the feathers off.

Charlie worked for us for quite a while. He slept in a bedroom on the second floor of our home. The going wage for a hired man then was twenty-five dollars a month plus room and board. His personal hygiene left something to be desired, and Nana hoped that different arrangements could be made. I talked with Charlie, and he agreed to our building a one-room cabin on skids. It didn't take long, and soon he moved into a new home that had a bed, a stove, and limited kitchen facilities, happy as a child with a new toy. Some of his family lived across the state border in eastern Ohio. I don't ever remember him asking for some time to go and pay a visit, but we offered to take him over. Carolyn was fourteen, and Danny was just a baby. The five of us left early one morning. Along the way we stopped, and Nana spread out a blanket on some nice, shady, green grass, and we had a picnic.

I talked with someone in the hospital at Union City, and they found a source of available funds that would provide medical care for Charlie's issues. After a little coaxing, he agreed to go and have surgery. Several days in the hospital in a bed with clean sheets and someone to bring his food should have been a highlight in his life. But he was very anxious to get back to his little cabin. We would supply his food that he served himself, or he would come and eat at our table. Obviously, he would spend some time in convalescing, but would come into the barn every morning while I was doing the milking and visit. He would always take a quart of fresh milk with him. No longer was there evidence of the large bulge in his jeans. He seemed to be in better health and was always happy. One morning he didn't show up. When I went to his cabin I found that during the night he had passed away. I was a pallbearer at his funeral. So ends the saga of Charlie Lord.

As time progressed, we bought a Ford 8N tractor, a different used car, a manure spreader, and a big chest freezer. The milking effort was difficult. Milk sold from two-fifty to three dollars a hundredweight, and we were struggling as was everyone else around us. We purchased about one hundred acres of vacant land about four miles from us that had quite a bit of timber on it. I still had the old sawmill, but it would have been difficult to move. We bought a new Frick sawmill made in York, Pennsylvania, in the southeastern part of the state. We also bought a used Minneapolis-Moline 100 HP power unit and set it up on the land purchased. Of course, chainsaws were in vogue by then, and we had one of those. Being somewhat younger then than I am now, I would get up and do the morning milking and clean the barn. Then hitch up the team to the pung (a sort of sled with sides that had a seat and space to carry some things), go the four miles and cut and skid logs to the mill all day, then back home and do the milking. There were quite a few ash trees on the property that I sold directly to a manufacturer in Union City that only used ash to make all kinds of handles. That was better than making lumber out of it. This project made a little money to help, but not a lot. Then we sold that property.

We had some timber on our farm, and most of it would make pulpwood. The premier paper of choice was manufactured in Erie. The name of the company was Hammermill Bond. Their trademark on their product was the name of the company watermarked into each sheet of paper. They, of course, bought hardwood by the cord. A cord measures four by four by eight feet. The eight-foot length of the pieces had to be cut at fifty inches. I hauled quite a number of loads into Erie. Now I understand that Hammermill Bond no longer is in business.

Like other struggling dairymen in the area, it was necessary to get some outside employment to earn enough money to buy feed for the cows so they would produce more milk for us to lose more money on. I worked on a road construction job for a while. It became known that they needed a night watchman. I applied for it and was successful. But I didn't tell them that I had a job working days for eight hours on the construction site. For a short time I handled both jobs, then one night the owner of the construction company drove up beside my car and found me sound asleep. I was fired from both jobs. Which was, of course, what I deserved. Then "Henny Penny's sky fell in." The state of Pennsylvania decided to test all the dairies in the state for brucellosis. That is a disease that causes abortion in cattle and can cause undulant fever in humans. Most of our thirty-plus cows tested positive and had to be sold for hamburger. The rest we sold at public auction right on the farm. It was a heavy loss, to be sure.

I always wanted some sheep, so we bought about 300 head and planned to use most of the farmland for pasture. The county extension service had a sheep shearing school, so I became educated in that trade and sheared all of our own sheep.

Our two younger children were growing up, and Robert Daniel Rotthoff II had started school. The school board of the Lowville School, of which I was a member, and the Erie church school board went into partnership and bought a building near Hamett, which was about halfway between Lowville and Erie. That is where he spent the first several years of school.

Making Ends Meet

Our financial needs still needed some attention and quite by Providence, I learned that Bascom Church Furniture in Keene, Texas, was looking for a sales representative in the east. I communicated with R.E. Bascom, owner of the company, and he invited me to come and interview. I took the job, and over the next seven years became a close friend of R.E., as he was known. This began my traveling years.

I became the sales manager for everything east of the Mississippi, and these years turned out to be happier and more satisfying years, as Nana and the children were able to make many trips with me. My employment with Bascom actually began earlier than I indicated because Danny was not in school yet for the first several years. When we traveled together, we would stay at boarding houses along the way. There were no motels then, a few cabins in some areas, and of course, there were small hotels in every small town and villages. But boarding houses were usually clean and well-kept, and the family could stay for from two to four dollars. I am sure that the "Bed and Breakfast" concept grew out of the boarding house of long ago.

Our home still had the old party line phone service with four long rings, and all calls to or from anyone who was not on our party line had to be connected by the operator through the central office in Wattsburg. I was in Virginia when I was able to contact a church in Holton, Maine. All the phone contacts with home and clients had to be made from public phones, which were placed here and there on street corners, most every-where. And most often calls were needed to be made when the sun was beating down in ninety-degree temps or the wind was blowing snow and it was below zero, all the while encased in a small glassed-in prison.

The folks in Holton were going to have a meeting to decide on church furniture the coming Monday night. Holton is in the very most northern part of Maine, just a mile from the New Brunswick border. So I called Nana and told her that I had checked the airlines and Mohawk had a flight the next day from Erie to Albany, New York. I asked her to meet me there, and after the meeting in Holton, we would travel home through Canada along the St. Lawrence Seaway, which had only recently been opened for ocean ships to travel into the Great Lakes.

So began a most memorable trip. She barely made it in time to the airport to get on the plane. Those planes were the old DC-3s, and they were the size of the planes we jumped from in the service. Danny was three, and Dawnie was just a tiny baby. There was a businessman across the aisle who was very kind and aided Nana when she needed a little help. She experienced some air sickness. The plane arrived safe and only a little late, and when it continued on to its next destination it took with it all of Nana's luggage, including diapers and baby food. But no matter, we were all together and happy, and in a little while, Marge was feeling much better.

Some incidents of the trip stand out in my memory. One: the two diapers that traveled with us, one because Dawn was wearing it and the other just happened to be in a carryon bag that Nana had. When one diaper became soiled, Nana would wash it at a filling station stop and hold it out the window to dry. Two: on a stop we purchased some milkshakes and Danny, standing behind my seat in the station wagon, spilled it down the back of my neck. But all in all, it was a good trip. We made it to the church meeting and was successful in obtaining the order for the pews and chancel furniture. We crossed over into New Brunswick and drove along the newly opened St. Lawrence Seaway. We came into a small town in Quebec and went into a small grocery store. Everything was not out for easy visual access, and the proprietor spoke no English, and we spoke no French. After several attempts to have him understand "milk," Nana said "moo, moo." With a big smile on his face, he said "ahh," and trotted behind some shelves and brought out a bottle of milk.

Bud wanted to go on a short trip with me one time when I would only be gone a couple of nights. We checked into a hotel in a small town in northern Pennsylvania. Then a room could be available for two or three dollars a night. The rooms were rather large, the ceilings high, and the light was on a cord from the ceiling with a chain you pulled to turn it on and off. The restroom and bath was down the hall. All the doors down the hall looked the same except for a different number on each one. Bud went down to use the restroom, and I was sure that he would not remember what our room number was. So when he went out, I locked the door. Presently, he came back and did try to gain access to the right door. When I was just a little boy, grandparents Pop and Mom had nicknamed me Toady. As the years went by, Bud always called me Tope. So outside that door, in somewhat of a loud whisper he said "Tope, Tope." I attempted to assume a woman's voice and loudly stated, "Honey, someone is trying to get in our door."

> *After several attempts to have him understand "milk," Nana said "moo, moo." With a big smile on his face, he said "ahh," and trotted behind some shelves and brought out a bottle of milk.*

When our Lowville church board decided to join with the Erie church and transport the children to a central location that would serve both churches, it was decided that the school building in Lowville would be renovated into a church. And so it was. Nana and I had the privilege of donating the pews and chancel furniture. (51) Many years later, I visited there and was so pleased that the church has been perfectly cared for, the grounds are well taken care of, and the interior looks just as it did then, away back in the 1950s. They remain in my prayers.

So the years kept drifting by. My friend R.E. Bascom decided to sell the church furniture business, and a firm from Los Angeles by the name of Brandon Cabinets bought him out. In less than a year they decided to get out of the church furniture business. So, after considerable thought, Nana and I decided we would start manufacturing church furniture in

Pennsylvania. I had many contacts in the east, and the fact is that most of the quality lumber used for church furniture is red and white oak, found chiefly in the northeast.

The Home Economics building as part of the many structures on the grounds of the Wattsburg Fairgrounds with a square footage space in excess of 10,000 feet, was vacant fifty weeks out of the year. It had three-phase electrical current and was located in a good geographical location. I proposed that the Fair board rent that facility to us. We would move our machines out of the way and shut down our operation for a vacation two weeks out of the year at fair time, which was around Labor Day. The plan was accepted. Jamestown, New York, was only thirty miles from Wattsburg and was the center of major furniture manufacturing. Several woodworking machinery dealers operated from there. So I made a list of the equipment that would be needed in our operation. The need included quality and heavy-duty equipment costing many thousands of dollars. Straight-line rip saw, heavy duty planers, cut-off saws, gluing racks, and equipment capable of gluing seat, back, and pew ends together. Some pew lengths were sixteen and eighteen feet. Cabinet-building equipment including many hand tools. Finish room equipment and material handling equipment. Desks, file cabinets, and office equipment.

As would be expected, it turned out to be a major undertaking. Some financing was available, and credit arrangements fell into line. The name chosen for the company was "Ecclesiastical Furniture, Inc." Additionally, we bought a truck for delivery and had the printing boldly displayed.

We were in business. The fair office was turned over to us for use. Catalogs, business cards, and promotional aids were printed. Specifications for the products were established.

The farm, including our home, was sold to the Pennsylvania Fish and Game Department. Some tears were shed, and many memories were tucked away. We moved to a rented home just north of Lowville.

Looking back, things went very well. We were producing a finished product of excellent value, and furnishing churches throughout the East. Then as fair time drew close, we were successful in purchasing the old tannery in Corry. (52) A quality set of buildings with plenty of room for expansion. So before the fair was to begin, we were successful in getting all of our equipment and inventory moved into the new quarters. We produced an attractive brochure announcing the move and change of location.

After being in Corry for about a year, it seemed important to have an airplane, as most of the travel demands for me were to the East Coast. We purchased a Piper Tri-Pacer. (38) It was the first year Piper came out with putting the new 160 HP Lycoming engine in their Tri-Pacer. The plane had four seats, a full panel, an auto-pilot, LF radio directional radio, and two Omni HF transmitters and receivers. I used it extensively in the business. Of course, the Aeronca I had during our courtship and early marriage years had been sold.

Somewhere along the line Margie and I decided to take a vacation. Together we had been on many trips to many places and had seen many wonders, but for the most part, they were all business trips. This time we were going to make it a vacation with no business. My mother would watch Danny, and Margie's sister in Greensburg, east of Pittsburgh, would keep Dawn, who I think was four or five years old. We headed for Orlando, Florida, dropping Dawn off in Greensburg. It was in the winter, but good flying weather. In the afternoon we were near Asheville, North Carolina, and for a while had neglected to pull on the carburetor heat. It iced up, and the engine began to stutter. There was a small airport nearby, and while trying to get the engine restarted, I circled over the airport. We had been flying at over seven thousand feet, so I had a little time. The engine came to life, and we continued on our way. We had a few days of Florida sunshine and relaxing at the pool. We visited some historical sites like St Augustine, then headed back north to the "salt mine." Up to that time, I had never had any adverse flying experiences, but there was one in the works.

It was in the late afternoon that we arrived at Greensburg to pick up Dawn. Ruth brought Dawnie to meet us at the airport. After a short visit and a check of the weather along our route of travel, we left with Dawn in the back seat where she fell asleep shortly after take-off. By the time we got away, it was dark, but the airport was lighted and had a rotating beacon. The weather report that I had was for good conditions along our route of travel with a snowstorm approaching from the west to arrive close to midnight. The report indicated that snow was then approaching Youngstown. Our flight plan indicated a little over an hour to Jamestown, N.Y. where we had left our car.

About halfway into our fight plan we began to encounter some snow showers, and in just a few minutes we were in and out of some pretty heavy, wet snow. We only had visual contact with the ground on and off. So, I made a 180-degree change in direction and headed back to Greensburg. It was then that I made the only radio contact with the emergency radio frequency in all my flying experience. The contact was made with the Allegany County Airport, which was the only commercial air facility for Pittsburgh. This was before they built the Greater Pittsburgh Airport a few years later.

After giving the operator our position and the flight condition, he advised us to take a heading to Pittsburgh where he could guide us in after we were close enough to show up on his radar. He said they were expecting snow to begin there shortly. Pittsburg was maybe forty or fifty miles west of our flight location. So I needed to make a decision. We offered a short prayer and asked to be guided. I gave him our ETA at Greensburg and told him that if we did not make contact with the rotating beacon at that time, we would take a heading for Allegheny County. He replied, "OK, but you may be making a mistake." Although I had some instrument training, I was not yet licensed to fly in instrument conditions. The heavy snow would build up on the leading edge of the wings and then sluff off with a chug.

It turned out that the decision was a good one. We came out of a cloud and could see a few cars on the highway, and just at the time expected, we saw the rotating beacon. I radioed our contact and told him we were in the landing pattern at Greensburg. God does indeed answer prayers. Don't you agree? The next day the weather permitted us to travel on to our destination.

Plane Talk

For any who read this that may have an interest in flying, I will attempt to recount a few items of interest reaching back to the Tri-Pacer era. I really did have a love affair with that airplane. I liked everything about it. It's N number was "niner-seven-one-one-Delta." VOR directional aids had only been developed and were still being put into operation, and the Tri-Pacer was equipped with that modern and favorable advantage. It also had a LF radio range receiver that was well known at that time as the A&N directional aid. It worked well but had some limitations that was largely overcome by Omni. Believe it or not it also had an auto-pilot.

The directional aids were important to me since our home and the plant were at Corry, Pennsylvania, pretty much to the western part of the state, and quite often it was necessary for me to have meetings with church committee meetings on the eastern seaboard. Those meetings were nearly always evening meetings, after which, weather permitting, I would fly home. Central Pennsylvania has the Allegheny Mountain range that is a pretty lonesome hundred miles or more. On the eastern edge is a fair-sized city named Williamsport, that had a VOR transmitter, and commercial airport with a tower. So I would always stop there. In those days I could request the tower's permission for me to come up and check the weather information across the mountains, also see if there were any pilot reports of adverse flying conditions. A time or two, because of the information available, I would go down to the first floor and stretch out on some seats, sleep a little, and wait for daylight. If the weather appeared acceptable, I would take a heading for Bradford where there was an airport and a VOR. Bradford is almost to the western edge of the mountains and is close to the upstate New York border. Then I'd go into Jamestown, where in anticipation I would have left my car.

One time, and only one time, I did not have auto transportation at Jamestown. I called Nana and gave her an ETA at the Corry airport, where there were no lights, and asked her to meet me and drive to the end of the grass and have her headlights on. She was there, as expected. I had to make two low passes while trying to fix my landing lights on the wind sox. I made it on the second pass and landed. I taxied to the hanger, and Nana and I put the plane to bed. We just got started down the road to town (the airport was just above the city) when there was a police car with their emergency lights on came up to the airport. We just continued on home. The next day there was a story in the paper that an airplane was having trouble, but the police were unable to find any problem.

It must have been about 1958 that I took Nana to the Washington Hospital in Takoma Park, Maryland, where she had a hernia removed from her tummy. While there, she made friends with a young nurse in training. Carmela had been sponsored into the United States from Peru by a doctor who had spent some time there as a missionary. When we were leaving, Carmela helped us down to the car, and Nana gave her a little tip and a hug.

Sometime later, she got in touch with Nana and asked if we would be willing to sponsor her boyfriend to come to America. So we jumped through all the hoops, and finally one day Nana went to Erie and picked up Manuel Sanchez. And so began an interesting lifetime friendship. Interesting to be sure. He knew no English, and we knew no Spanish. But he came to live with us in our home and worked for us in the factory. It was a good educational experience for Danny and Dawn, and for all of us. Slowly he began to understand us, and we began to understand him. He had a good singing voice and would sometimes sing a solo in Spanish in our little church.

He and Carmela courted by mail and phone, with a personal visit or two and soon decided to get married. They were married in the Washington Sanitarium and Hospital Chapel, and I gave Carmela away at the ceremony. (92, 93) He became involved in the ownership of a furniture recovering and draperies business and Carmela an in-demand registered nurse. Years later they followed us to Idaho where we maintain our family relationship. They are now both retired. A little nostalgic memory of yesteryear.

Some things just seem to stand out as I allow my mind to drift back in time. Last night I lay awake remembering how I traveled away from the farm and my family, Nana and the children, so much a part of my life. This brought to my mind a song from the mid-1970s by John Denver called "Back Home Again." The sentiment fit perfectly … back home again.

The next three years produced many high points and valleys. We furnished many churches, grew to have an employment level of near fifty. We were producing a quality line of furnishings and always had a backlog of orders. But we struggled with inadequate capital. Unfortunately, I did not have good business ability. I seemed to have some sales ability, but lacked the ability to deal with the rough and tumble characteristics of dealing with bankers and promoters and other hardline businessmen of the world. So, in 1961 we got out from under it and began a different lifestyle. There were and remain a lot of interesting memories connected with the ten years in the church furniture business. Some years later R.E. Bascom went back into the business and came to visit us in California wanting me to join him and manage the sales. But unfortunately, I was deeply involved in sales and marketing with another company.

Alan Fisher was CEO and owner of the Ace Drill Bushing Company in La Sierra, California. He had a relative there in Wattsburg with whom he came to visit one time, and we were introduced. That was at the time we were operating out of the fairgrounds. Our neighbor from Wattsburg told him that we were getting out of the business. He called and said that he had just purchased one of his competitors and offered to move us to Glendale, California, if I would become the market and sales manager of All American Drill Jig Bushing Company.

Margie and I talked about it and decided to go. We placed our furniture in storage in Erie. This was before the travel trailer industry was really getting underway. We were able to buy an older eight-foot-wide house trailer. Carolyn's husband, Art, who had served as the plant manager for us all the time we were in charge of the manufacturing business, was a very talented workman. It was he that helped us to make a travel trailer and home on wheels out of that purchase.

California, Here We Come

Saying goodbyes to family and friends is always a drain on emotions. We were beginning a new venture three thousand miles away. Carolyn and Art wanted to go in that direction, and we promised to look for an opportunity for them when we arrived. Dawn was in second grade, and that would have put Danny in grade four. They were a good age for traveling, and they traveled well. So we hitched up to our "covered wagon" with our 1960 Ford station wagon and headed out on a cold winter day. The trip was reminiscent of the covered wagons pulled by real "horse power" or "oxen power" to California destinations. Perhaps we should have taken the initiative to keep a daily log, but I don't think we ever thought about it. Along the way, there were some points of interest that have remained quite vivid in our minds. For about the first time in our life, we were not bound to keep any kind of a schedule.

Because it was December, we chose to travel the southern route through Kentucky, which was where Nana spent a number of years as a child. She was born in Uniontown, Pennsylvania, where her father worked as a telephone lineman. She had three brothers, Lewis who was a year older than she, then Eugene a couple of years her junior, and last was Glen who was about seven or eight years younger (102) than Nana. So that everyone knows, Nana's maiden name was Margaret Elizabeth Adams. Her father's name was Alvin Adams, and her mother's was Cora. (47) Too bad she is not here at this writing to provide an accurate historical record of her growing up years, but the year of this project is 2017, and it was eleven years ago on June 18, 2006, that she passed away.

Her father fell from a telephone pole when Margie was perhaps ten years old and was incapacitated for some time. I think he did go back to work for a while, but some time along the line the family decided to move back to where her father's family was in the area of Winchester, Kentucky, not far from the Bluegrass country of Lexington. When Margie was twelve, her father passed away, and within a year or so her mother decided to bring the family back to Pennsylvania. I think at that time they moved to Greensburg.

Some years later, maybe five or six, her mother married Mr. Bair, a somewhat older man who was the head elder of the local Seventh-day Adventist Church in Greensburg. I understood him to be a very fine and kind gentleman. He and Nana's mother had one daughter named Ruth. At this writing, all of Margie's brothers have passed away, and the family has lost track of Ruth.

Now we must get back to our odyssey that is underway from northwestern Pennsylvania to Glendale, California. We got waylaid a little in Kentucky. In the western part of that state, we paid a visit to some well-known caves that at one time provided hiding places and shelter for some big-name outlaws of yesteryear. Then, on to the state of Arkansas. Which, by the way, so that you know, is the only state in America that is mentioned in the Bible. "and Noah looked out of the 'ark and saw'."

We arrived in West Texas at El Paso where Margie had a cousin named Bob who, with his wife and two children about the same age as Danny and Dawn, owned and operated a large cotton farm, not far from the Rio Grande River and the Mexican border. I had received word that I needed to make a trip back to sign some papers dealing with the closing of the business in Pennsylvania. This worked out ideally. Margie and the children stayed in the trailer parked on the cotton farm, and I flew to Erie and took care of that business matter. I think I returned the next day and we spent several days becoming acquainted with raising cotton. I remember Bob and family took us up to Las Cruces, New Mexico, to visit that historic city. We ate at some famous Mexican restaurant and forever after would enjoy food from south of the border. Bob and Betty Adams and Nana and I visited back and forth several times during the years of our California sojourn.

Leaving El Paso, our journey through New Mexico, Arizona, and into California did not make any significant memories. The evening we approached Los Angeles it was raining hard, it was dark, and the road was overloaded with California traffic, of which we were unaccustomed to. But God carried us on through to our destination safely. It must have been suggested to us that we look for living quarters in Glendale or up in the near part of the San Fernando Valley. We found a place to park and crawled into our covered wagon. So our first night in California became history.

The next day we found a new apartment with a swimming pool that had just opened to rent. The address was 2722 Honolulu Avenue which ever after the kids put into a song and would sing "2722 Honolulu Avenue." We will never forget that address. Nana, being the professional swimmer that she was, was so pleased, which made the transition of our move so much easier. We parked the covered wagon in the parking lot and put a for sale sign on it. In just a few days Nana had it sold.

We registered both Danny and Dawnie in the La Crescenta Seventh-day Adventist School. It must have had forty or fifty children attending. It was located several miles from our home at the church, where we transferred our membership. Because of the busy streets and highways, Nana would have to provide the transportation to and from school. The school principal, Kenneth Ackerman and his wife Joyce, have kept in contact with us for so many years. Before we left California, they had transferred to a large school in northern California where he served as principal. Then when they had retired, they would visit us in Garden Valley for a good many years. They made their home in Acampo, California. When Nana passed away after we had been in Garden Valley for over forty years, and I went to Alaska as a volunteer missionary pilot and served as lay pastor of the Togiak Church, they still kept in contact with me. Even after Ken passed away, Joyce and I maintained contact.

All American Drill Bushings was located in Glendale, seven or eight miles from our home. Alan Fisher took into the ownership of the company when he bought it Nathan Shaw, who had been a valuable employee of Ace Drill Bushings for many years. Nathan was the president of All American and was who I reported to. He and his wife Margaret and Nana and I became good friends.

So you will understand the nature of the product All American manu-factured, it is a very precision instrument used in industry to guide a drill. As industrial manufacturers develop a product, jigs are made to guar-antee that every part of the airplane or automobile or heavy machinery or whatever, that needs an original part or that will ever need that part replaced, will fit exactly. These drill guides are part of the jig that guide the drill in making the hole to very exact locations. The drill bushings are manufactured to a normal tolerance of two- to three-thousandths of an inch. But on special orders can be made with tolerances to ten-thousandths of an inch. As you can imagine, there would be required machinists and inspectors who understand and have the ability to meet these standards.

It was my responsibility to develop a marketing plan and see that it was put into action. We marketed through industrial supply houses in every industrial geographical area of the United States. This was a new chal-lenge for this young country boy. I had had no background in the product; I had no background with this kind of industry and with industrial sup-ply houses. Woodworking and milking cows supplied directly to the con-sumer. About the only similarity was that both required almost constant travel. In the next few years, United Airlines awarded me a Million Miler recognition. Of course, that included miles traveled on other airlines also.

Usually, I would spend Monday in the office then be gone until Friday. The men I worked for were truly great. We worked out a plan where I could take my family with me from the time school let out in the spring until it started the day after Labor Day in the fall. Nana and I developed a plan that first year where we purchased a very nice wall tent from Sears that served as our home for the next two summers. We also purchased the cooking and other necessary equipment. Then away we went all over the United States.

We would find a state or national park, set up camp, then early in the morning I would don a suit and white shirt and work the industrial supply houses of the city of choice. Then I'd come back to camp and enjoy the family, perhaps swim in a lake. Take a hike or just listen to the kids tell of their accomplishments through the day. If the city was a large one, we might stay in the same location for another day or two. Sometimes if I had selected a supply house to represent us and the owner or president would allow me to take him out for dinner, I would tell him I had my family with me, and I would suggest that he bring his and we have dinner all together. This would sometimes develop into friendships that lasted for years.

A very nice campground near Houston, Texas, produced a memorial experience. When I came back that evening, the kids had made friends with a large, beautiful furry monkey. The monkey was owned by the camp manager. Somewhere there is a picture of Danny with the monkey on his shoulder. The next year we went back to the same camp but was told that the monkey had died. There was a very nice campground near Dallas and I think we were there over a weekend. One Sunday there were some families who had a large nice boat and offered get us into water skiing. That was a totally new experience for our whole family.

As we neared New Orleans from the north on a hot night, we saw a couple of possums, which were new to the kids as well as new to Nana, I assured them that they were not new to me, because I trapped them in Pennsylvania, though their fur was not worth near the value of skunks and muskrats. It was after dark when I pulled into a filling station, a bright light on a pole, flooding the area with light that was attracting all kinds of night-flying insects. Some or all the insects were killed by the heat, or whatever, and lay under the light on the ground. There was a quantity sufficient to cause the wheel to skid when a little brake was applied.

Getting some direction to the location of a campground we continued. Presently, it was evident that there was a large body of water on our right and soon we turned in that direction to the bridge crossing what turned out to be Lake Pontchartrain. This has to be the longest bridge in the world. I don't remember the length in miles, but it must have been twenty or more. Two lanes, one going in each direction. I do remember that it went on and on. Finally, we reached the other side and found the campground. It was late, and we were all very tired. The temp must have been 100 degrees, hot and muggy. Well that all happened fifty-five years ago, and I'm sure things have changed a lot, but I bet the bugs are still around and the temp remains at 100 degrees with the humidity at 100 percent.

We had a few days and determined to visit the old city, feeling quite sure that we would not be back again as a family, although I did set up a distributor and made business trips back over the next few years. One interesting factor that has forever stuck in our minds was the custom, or perhaps the need, to bury the dead above ground. We visited a cemetery with numerous masonry structures in which the dead were laid on bunks, and after decomposition took place, their bones could be scraped off, and another body takes its place. I understand that the water table is close to the land surface making grave burial impossible.

> *We visited a cemetery with numerous masonry structures in which the dead were laid on bunks, and after decomposition took place, their bones could be scraped off, and another body takes its place.*

The summer of 1962 with all of its interesting and challenging days was moving on. We traveled to some of the industrial spots in the northern tier of the United States and on to the Seattle area, a heavy industrial city with Boeing Aircraft and a host of other companies of reputation. It happened that the World's Fair was on, and this offered a unique educational opportunity for Danny and Dawn. We found a camp spot in a very busy location and set up our tent. Earlier in the year, I had already set up Aaron's Industrial as a distributor, so after visiting with them part of the day, we spent some time at the fair. I think the high point was our visit to the Space Needle. We did not eat in the restaurant at the top of the Needle. It was being patronized by a lot of people and prices were high compared with other locations. So after a couple of days, we packed up our camp and headed home. It was a good summer.

We had signed a lease for a year on the apartment at 2722 Honolulu Avenue, and though it had been a great place to live and the owners had treated us very well, we really did need more space. We found a house on Rockdell Street, the last street up against the mountain. From there on it was steep. It was a brand-new home having just been built by the couple who lived right in front. They had purchased a large lot and built this home. No landscaping had been done. It had four bedrooms, two baths, and a large living room with an attractive fireplace open on three sides. It had a two-car garage. We planted some trees and made it look attractive. It was a good place to live.

Next door to us lived Boyd and Katie Davis. Their daughter Kelty became and remains a lifelong very close friend to Dawn. Katie was an artist of considerable repute, and Boyd had an import business. We became lifelong friends. A couple of years Boyd went with me elk hunting in Idaho. Both Boyd and Katie have passed away now.

Hunting and Camping Adventures

The first year that Boyd Davis went hunting with me, he took a nice cow elk early the first day of our hunt. The second year he went with me, it turned out to be an altogether different circumstance. Danny went on the hunt with us also. About the third day of the hunt, we were riding into our camp on Sack Creek when Danny and Boyd decided to race. I yelled, "You guys better be careful." They were less than a hundred yards from camp when Boyd's horse made a quick turn, putting him leaning somewhat to the right of vertical, he threw his arm up over his chest as he came into contact with a tree.

He lay on the ground in pain, as Danny and I managed to carry him into the tent, got him in his sleeping bag, and built a fire. A doctor friend of mine had given me a prescription grade painkiller to put into my first aid kit. I gave him one of them, and soon he felt well enough to remind me that I had given him a long discourse of the value and benefits of a product called Bag Balm that was used extensively in the cow milking business and its value for a great variety of uses. He said with somewhat of a sleepy grin, "Dan, get the Bag Balm." I gave Danny some last-minute instructions to keep the fire in the stove going, and I left on Ringo.

It was about six miles to where our vehicles were, then a drive of about six or eight miles to the Elk Creek Ranger Station. The man in charge there radioed out and had a helicopter dispatched from Garden Valley. When he landed at Elk Creek, I got in with him and directed him to the camp. There was an opening about 200 yards from the camp large enough to land. There was a stretcher fastened to the landing frame on the outside, and we carried it to the camp, loaded Boyd in it in his sleeping bag, and the three of us carried him to the helicopter. Two straps fastened him and the gurney to the landing frame, but the one that would go over his chest had to be placed lower over his stomach because of his fractured wrist and ribs.

It was getting dark when the helicopter lifted very slowly and turned with a light showing his distance from the trees. When he reached well above the elevation of trees, he began a horizontal flight. Later Boyd told me that the airflow when that horizontal change was made, ballooned his bedroll to the point that he was sure he was going leave the helicopter. But the straps held and the flight continued. The equipment used then in the 1960s was altogether different than what is used now.

It was dark, and the pilot was afraid to fly over the summits out of Bear Valley. So he radioed Elk Creek and told them that he would set down along the road. They brought a pickup that had no canopy and loaded my poor hunting partner in the back of the pickup, then drove him about forty miles over very rough roads to Lowman, where an ambulance carried him on to Boise. The next day I went to visit him in the hospital. Amazingly, his attitude and spirits were high. Some different than I'd expected. They remained high for the rest of his life. He was indeed a real gentleman with a great personality. The next hunting season he and his wife Katie, Nana and I used the same camp on Sack Creek and had an especially wonderful time together.

During the winter of 1962–63 we purchased a new travel trailer. It was a Santa Fe. It slept six and had a small refrigerator and stove. Had an overhead bed that extended over the front of the towing vehicle. Pretty nice, and it served us well for several years.

After being on the road for a number of days, we were traveling through Wyoming. It was before they had built the freeway in that part of the country, so the highway traveled through the towns. In Laramie we decided to stop and buy some groceries. Just off the main street was the county courthouse and other county buildings and just a short distance was a market. So we parked in front of the courthouse where there was a beautiful lawn. The children did not want to go shopping and said that they would just sit there on the grass.

There was next to no moving traffic. Nana and I had headed for the store when a young man came out of a side street too fast; maybe he was under the control of a drink or two. The left front of his car came into the side of our new trailer right where the wheel was. Didn't blow the tire and did very little damage to the trailer body, but it bent the axel. I don't remember all the details, but the police came and at least made a report. Our traveling was put on hold. I called the manufacturer in Los Angeles, and they shipped us a new axel by air. We either had it the next day or the second day and was again on our way east.

One night we were all sound asleep when a gurgling sound awakened me. For some reason, the thought came into my mind that it was blood flowing out of an artery. WOW, what a dumb impression. What happened was our little refrigerator was set too cold. The glass milk bottle had frozen enough that it broke the bottle and let the rest of the liquid gurgle out onto the floor.

No doubt the most dramatic incident that we faced in the years that we traveled as a family across the United States occurred as we neared the end of the summer of 1963. The last city in which to take care of business was Salt Lake City, and then we planned to visit Bryce Canyon National Park, before heading home to La Crescenta. In the evening or during the night, Dawn was suffering some acute stomach discomfort. So in the morning, I asked my distributor for the name of a pediatrician. He gave me the name of the one he and his family used and even called and made an appointment. The doctor, after examining Dawn, said it was not serious and recommend we give her some coke syrup.

The next day we traveled on to Bryce Canyon. We camped at a campground near the park headquarters. Sometime after midnight, the pain in Dawn's abdomen became a critical emergency, and we took her to the main lodge where a nurse was on duty. By that time the pain had subsided, and she thought all was okay but advised us to go to the hospital to make sure. It was a small hospital in Panguitch.

It must have been two or three in the morning when Dr. Duggins came into the little ten-bed hospital that was a renovated home. His initial appearance did not exude much confidence. He could be described as a typical country doctor. I remember being impressed with the cow manure on his boots. After his brief examination, he stated positively that Dawn had appendicitis and that it had already ruptured. That she must have emergency surgery now. The operating room would be prepared, and early that morning, in that small western Utah community, we had no choice but to turn her over to this unimpressionable country doctor and pray that God would guide his action and save our daughter's life.

How long the surgery lasted, I cannot remember. But I remember her coming to the recovery area and not looking like there was much life within her. Since all the ten beds in the hospital were occupied, they had to set up another bed for her in a hallway. She was there for the next ten days, and either Nana or I would stay with her. Our trailer was in the parking lot of the hospital, and we were back and forth between the two points. One day I took Danny, and we traveled on some back-country roads in the area.

The days slowly passed by, and we found out that it would be necessary for Dawn to have some bowel action before she would be released. The surgical procedure had required a considerable effort to remove the infected material from the abdominal cavity where it had been distributed within the intestinal tract. In removing the infected material from around the intestines, it required careful action so as not to disturb any more than necessary, but even a small about of disturbance could interfere with bowel action. So we waited and prayed. Then one day, one of the nurses heard the passage of some gas, and it was that event that produced a celebration among the hospital staff and their willingness to return our daughter to us. Praise the Lord, we were on our way home.

For several years after we remembered to send gifts and cards to Dr. Sims E. Duggins. So is proven that we should not pass judgment on anyone, based on the evidence of what is seen, including the cow manure on their boots. This man was truly a classic individual with extraordinary medical ability. Also, this experience has proven that God does indeed answer prayer. Your prayers can and will be answered also if you put your faith and trust in Him. Take the time to study what these terms, faith and trust, mean.

It may have been the winter of 1963–64 that we decided to make a trip to Mexico in our Santa Fe trailer. We went to Mazatlan, A city on the mainland at a point across the Bay of California from the southern tip of the Baja California peninsula. It was approximately 1,200 miles from our home in La Crescenta. We invited Bud and Sweetie to go along with us. They came out from Pennsylvania. They would occupy the bed in the overhead location, the kids in the bed that would be made up out of the kitchen table, and Nana and I in the bed in the rear of the crowded trailer. But it worked, and it turned out to be a memorable experience. With the tensions that have developed in the world today, I would not even consider such a journey.

The second night out, we pulled into a vacant gravel pit just off the highway, had our dinner and got ready for bed. Everyone had bedded down when a knock came at the door. I opened the door to find a soldier, who, in very broken English, told me that he and his companions would guard us through the night. I don't remember how he made known that some financial contribution would be appreciated, so I offered him a five-dollar bill. He expressed great appreciation. During the night I looked out a couple of times and saw four or five men on guard around a fire.

Upon arriving at our destination, we found very clean and comfortable camping accommodations. There was even a small American community nearby where some came and spent the winter in that tropical environment. Every day a Mexican man would come through with some freshly baked bread and rolls. Bud rationalized that the baking process would destroy any harmful bugs. The bread tasted very good, and I guess Bud was right because none of us ever became ill. A very nice beach was close by, but there was a warning that there were barracudas had infested the shoreline, so we did not get any swimming.

On the way home, we stopped in Hermosillo. I remember standing on the front entrance of a very lavish church, large and with luxurious appointments inside and out, and looking at the residential community nearby and being impressed with the abject poverty of the people.

It was a very good trip; educational and instructive in so many different ways. We were thankful that God provided us with a safe and trouble-free journey. I would however strongly advise against anyone making a similar trip in today's world.

Along about the next year we sold the Santa Fe and purchased a used 30-foot Airstream trailer, which served us well for the remainder of our life in California. From the first year in California, I went hunting elk in Idaho. That area became my destination every year and developed into such an important part of the lives of our whole family forever after.

There was an ad in an outdoor magazine that attracted my attention about some development in the old mining ghost town of Deadwood. We were returning home from a summer on the road and were camped on the upper Salmon River near Stanley. Looking at the map we were about sixty or seventy miles out of the way from visiting Deadwood. Danny was not interested in the trip, so we unhooked the trailer and left it at the campsite. Nana, Dawn, and I left early in the morning and went into the backcountry. All the old town was there and had been purchased from the Kellogg Mining Company by a man named Webb Appel.

It had been a silver and lead mining operation from near the turn of the century, but had blossomed into a major effort during World War II. There were about forty cabins, twenty-five or thirty in good condition. All had electric power with electric stoves and hot water tanks. Each also had good kitchen wood stoves and heating stoves for the cabins. They were two stories. There was a very nice lodge with a large double oven wood cookstove. There was also a building that had housed a sawmill plus other buildings, including the old mine mill with all its heavy crushing equipment, etc.

In Idaho every licensed outfitter operates his business within certain geographical areas. The outfitter in this area was Sterling Alley from Garden Valley. He had a deal with Appel and used the cabins and lodge for his business. There was also a corral for his horses and a tack room. It happened that Sterling was out on the trail with some clients. His daughter, Jan, and her husband were there. So it was with her that I made my reservations to hunt that fall. It was to be a "spike" hunt, where the outfitter would have set up a camp in which there were a tent and a stove and would have cut the firewood. We would provide all the other necessities for the hunt.

He would pack our supplies in, and we would ride in on horseback. He would check the camp in the middle of the week and take out any game we had taken, then at the conclusion of the week hunt, he would pack us out. The camp that we occupied was called the West Fork of Elk Creek, and it was about an eight-mile pack from the base camp at Deadwood. A friend and neighbor by the name of Allred was my hunting partner. I had taken a small buck deer; my partner had been unsuccessful, but we had a good time and a wonderful exposure to some wonderful country. Not another human being did we see during the week.

The next year Nana had experienced some severe back pain for some months. Part of the time she had been confined to bed and was required to wear a stiff brace. We had talked on a number of occasions about her accompanying me on my hunt. Though she was not inclined to be a huntress, she was indeed a good sport and loved the mountains. We both went in to visit the doctor. When I told him that she would like to go with me on a hunt, he reacted emphatically, "Absolutely not." Nana and I talked about it, and she decided to go in defiance to the doctor's advice. My hunting partner that year was Bob Spillers a man that operated a business manufacturing and supplying artificial arms and legs and was a member of our church.

Alley had suggested a camp known as "Sixteen to One Creek." It would be a horseback trip of about five miles from where we would leave our pickup. It was a beautiful September day, and Nana was wearing her large brace under a tee shirt. Part of the way, I rode behind her and noticed that every step that her horse made, I could see the muscles on either side of her spine flex. The trip in was good, and she had no regrets that she had come along. After a couple of days in camp, she removed the brace and never put it back on. She rode out of camp and felt better with a stronger back than ever. For years after that, if her back indicated some discomfort, she would ride a horse for a while and then she would be again free of pain. We have always felt very strongly that God somehow had led us into making the decision that we did. Remember, "God works in mysterious ways, His wonders to perform."

The hunt on Sixteen to One was successful for me. I took a nice four-point mule deer and a spike bull elk. I was seated on my old palomino horse Ringo when I spotted the bull, just standing there watching us. I slowly took my rifle out of the scabbard, took my feet out of the stirrups and fired. Then picking myself up off the ground, I got my steed who had just wandered a few yards away, and leading him, went into the brush. Sure enough there he was. The bullet had been well placed. It broke his neck. I dressed him out, found Bob, and the two of us loaded a half on each of our horses and led them into camp. Then both of my successes were hanging in camp, and that would make for a much easier pack for the outfitter. We hunted hard for Bob, but he was just not able to connect with anything. But he would hunt with me the next year. The buck I had mounted and it occupied a place on the wall of our homes until I moved to Alaska and served as a volunteer pilot many years later.

One time I went on a cougar hunt. After elk hunting I left our horses and the van I was driving in Garden Valley and booked a cougar hunt with Steve Alley, Sterling's son. He had a good set of hounds and had good success in hunting cats. I returned for the hunt in January.

With snowmobiles we spent several days searching for cougar tracks in deep snow, every day being unsuccessful. Then one day there was a fresh set of bobcat tracks going up the mountain on the Middle Fork of the Payette, I said, "OK, let's try at least for a bobcat." Several hours later after climbing into some pretty steep country on foot following the dogs, we heard them barking "treed." Sure enough, there near the very top of a Ponderosa pine was a beautiful bobcat that turned out it must be a lynx cross. It was light in color and had the lynx tufts on his ears.

Steve had instructed me that in hunting the big cats, a .22 pistol was all that was generally used. If a rifle of heavy caliber were used, the force of the bullet in striking bone would be more likely to knock the cat out of the tree, still much alive, and pose a problem to the dogs. Where the bullet from a .22 pistol was to be aimed to the location of the lungs, then in just a short time the cat would become weak and fall out of the tree. Since it was the head of the cougar that when measured was used to determine its competitive size, and any damage to the skull would disqualify it to be even considered.

But in the case of bobcats, they were not even considered as a game animal, and this one was not a good target as he looked down from his perch among the needles there halfway to the stars. It did take a few shots to dislodge him, and when he hit the ground, he was dead. So the trip and the hunt were at least partially successful. I was going to have to load the horses and head home the next day. Steve had gone out with his snow machine early, and as I was loading the horses, he returned with the news that he found a fresh cougar track. So with the dogs loaded and the snow machine, we headed up Lightning Creek, a tributary to the Middle Fork.

Just a few miles up, we put the dogs on the fresh set of tracks and listened as they bayed along the tracks. It wasn't long until the tone changed to that of sending a message to us, that the object of the hunt was up a tree. On our journey following the trail of the dogs and the cougar, we found where it had killed a buck deer and had eaten its lungs. We arrived at the tree, and contrary to the bobcat tree of the day before, this huge cat was up a relatively small lodgepole pine and was not more than twenty feet above the ground. Also, the limbs of the tree were small, and he was having trouble with balance in staying in the tree. Obviously, he had not used good judgment in selecting that one.

One shot from my pistol and about a minute of waiting, and he was on the ground, and the dogs were on the attack. It was only a short distance to a large Ponderosa pine. He had both front feet a couple of feet off the ground, and the dogs were working to prevent his escape when he fell over on his side dead. The .22 slug had done its work. Tragically, in the fight, he had managed, with the swipe of his talons to open a wide gap in one of the dog's side and some intestine was oozing out. It was one of Steve's best, and his most favorite dog. I told Steve to take the dogs and the wounded one back with the snowmobile, and I would skin the cat, and then put it in my backpack and walk on out.

It was just dark when I finished that task and loaded it in my pack. I, of course, did not skin out the head, the feet, or the tail, but would leave that for the taxidermist to do. That required some close and careful work. I could see that I was not far above Lightning Creek, and I knew how it had paralleled the trail somewhere down country. So, that is the direction in which I headed. Down on the creek, the going was pretty good. It was frozen over solid, or at least so I thought, and even though it was now dark, I could move right along. There was close to a foot of snow over the ice which gave me a good footing.

Then I got to thinking that there will be a place where, because of the water moving fast, or some other reason, the ice did not exist or would not hold me up. There was a vertical bank just above the water line, so I sat down and took off the backpack. With my flashlight, I found some dead needles, and in the top of a windfall, there were some small branches I could break off. I got a nice little fire going, leaned against my pack against the bank and was thinking of the success of this hunt when I heard the noise that represented the modern age that I lived in. Steve was coming back to save my life. He stopped all of a sudden and shut the noise off. He had smelled the smoke from my fire. He gave a yell, and I had no choice but to abandon the comfort and security of my new "home" and head back to civilization.

Both the bobcat and the cougar I took to a taxidermist in Glendale who had mounted a cow elk head for me (the big bull I had mounted in Boise). Both of the cats I had mounted life-size. The cougar skull I had measured after the required year where it was found to gain entrance into the Boone and Crockett record book. The Boone and Crockett record and the skull are displayed with the mount. There were so many memories, and many of them are still quite vivid in my mind. All of the trophies now occupy space in Dawn and Tom's lodge in Deadwood, but the memories I continue to carry along with me.

Here's another story about a trip that we as a family had made to Idaho. Danny had spent a year at Gem State Academy, and I had some business calls in Idaho and eastern Wyoming. I drove the Ditty Service truck with our horses and Nana drove the pickup with the Airstream. We set up camp about a half mile off the road in Bear Valley. I was around part of the time, but it was a long trip over to Afton, Wyoming.

Our camp was only about fifty yards from the creek where the Pacific salmon were spawning. Dawn had a girlfriend with her, and on an afternoon that I was gone, the two girls decided to sunbathe in an opening of the willows along the creek. Nana was in the Airstream and presently noticed a pickup pull up near the creek and two men get out. They both were in Fish and Game uniforms. The one with his head down and his hand on his sidearm snuck to where the girls were, the other was walking toward the trailer. Nana came to the door and yelled to the one sneaking into the willows to get out of there, that she had two young girls in there sunbathing. I don't know if he made it to the sunbathing site or not, Dawn will have to answer that, but he turned and headed back to the pickup, I would imagine rather sheepishly. The other man told Nana they were just checking on fishermen. Fishing during the spawning period was illegal. Nana assured him that there were no fishermen in this camp.

It happened that the one heading into the brush was Bill Pogue who later checked our outfitters camp on a fairly regular basis, and I got to know him quite well. He is the Bill Pogue that was killed by Claude Dallas along with another officer near the Idaho-Nevada border. There are two interesting books written on this story. Pogue was a small man that Dallas loaded into his pickup and took him to a location in the desert where he buried him. The other was a big man, and Dallas pushed him into a stream. He was later found.

It must have been that year that we bought four horses from Sterling and brought them to La Crescenta, where our neighbors, the Davises, invited us to keep them in their backyard, which was just across the fence from our backyard. I think there was one neighbor who registered a complaint because there was no other equine in the entire area, but they remained for the next few years until we left Southern California. Naturally, it meant that we must have the ability to transport these beautiful animals over the highways. We found a 20-year-old 1946 cab-over ton and half Ford truck that had been designed for government use to service radar sites and had for some years been owned by a furniture dealer in his business. We painted over the name, and the van-like vehicle became known and referred to by the kids as "Daddy's Ditty Service" (because it resembled a diaper delivery truck).

The neighbor on the other side of us whose name was also Davis (no relation to the Boyd Davises) was an accomplished mechanic, and we hired him to overhaul the old V8 engine in the "Ditty Service" truck. We cut a few small openings near the top of the van and put louvers in them to allow for some air movement. The large back door we replaced with a let-down ramp to load and unload the horses. We built a manger across the middle with a hinged section that would allow an opening whereby two or three horses could be taken to the front and turned around with their heads facing the back, then two or three could be loaded facing the front.

The van-like vehicle became known and referred to by the kids as "Daddy's Ditty Service."

That fall Bob Spillers went hunting with me again. We went to a different camp again. This time in Bear Valley on Cash Creek. The horses we had purchased and had left with Alley we took into camp and used them. Alley only furnished the packhorses and, of course, had set up the camp and cut the firewood. I had an elk whistle, and the first two days had some exciting exchanges with some bulls. The third day I used it to bring a nice big six point to within rifle range. He was big and it was a real job to get him dressed out and get the cape skinned out for the taxidermist. I had Sterling bring pack horses in to pack him out. Though I have used riding saddles to pack sometimes, it is much better to have the Decker packsaddles. That was an exciting trophy that hung on the wall in our home with the mule deer many years. Now all my trophies are displayed at Deadwood Outfitters Lodge which is owned and operated by Dawn and her husband Tom.

Now in this saga, must be told the adventure of using "Daddy's Ditty Service" to transport our new horses from Garden Valley, Idaho, to La Crescenta, California. Danny went with me. First was Ringo, the palomino I had used each year when going to Idaho; he and I had bonded well. Next was Suzie, a quarter horse cross that weighed 1,300 pounds that Nana had used on our trips together. Suzie was very gentle and suited Nana very well. For Danny, I had purchased Chile, a mare and a daughter of Suzie, tall and somewhat spirited, but gentle and easy to handle. For Dawn, I had purchased a gentle bay mare, but when arriving to pick the horses up, Sterling told me that she had become injured and would replace her with an attractive and gentle pinto mare. We loaded them up and was on our journey to their new home.

Somewhere along the way I called and told Nana that she and Dawn should come and meet us somewhere along the highway in the desert south of Mojave. We met, and I just pulled the Ditty Service van off on the side of the road and unloaded the pinto mare. I think seriously that the thrill registered with Dawn was to remain without a parallel for the rest of her life, as she was introduced to her very own horse. Later she named her Flicka, and they bonded together just as a girl and her horse should. After we had reloaded and were getting ready to finish the trip home, Nana told her that her hands smelled like horse and Dawn's reply was, "I'm never going to wash them again as long as I live."

Just across Rockdell Street, there was a small meadow encircled with timber and brush (manzanita), where we were free to take the horses and graze them at times. Right behind the meadow, the mountain rose quickly and steep. Just a little bit to the west of our place, the area was acceptable to the development of a subdivision. There were many good-sized eucalyptus trees, and I got permission to cut them for firewood. I bought a chainsaw, and Danny and I became involved in the firewood business.

We supplied a good inventory for ourselves, then sold a good many pickup loads within the community.

When we had a long weekend, we would load up the horses and travel north to a place called Three Rivers, where there was considerable open country to ride in and graze the horses. Just a beautiful place to camp and be out of the massive numbers of people there in Southern California. One time, Bud and Sweetie visited us, and we went up there for a weekend.

Of Horses, Cattle Drives, and a Youth Guest Ranch

Danny was to start high school, and we were planning to send him to Gem State Academy in Idaho. It was about that time that Nana and I felt the need for me to spend more time at home with the children rather than to be gone all week, almost every week, thus leaving the raising of the children largely up to her. So I gave Nathan and Alan notice of my plan. I told them that if necessary I would stay for as long as a year and aid in training someone to take my place. They did employ a man, but he didn't work out. The year was fast coming to an end, but they gave me their blessings when I left. Months later I stopped in to visit Nathan, and he took me up to my old office and asked if I would come back and move in.

I applied for a job with the Electric Storage Battery Company in their industrial division. The products handled were large fork-lift batteries, aircraft batteries, and emergency lighting batteries. No automotive batteries. The product name was Exide. I was to call on industries in Southern California and would be home almost every night. It went well for a couple of months, then they called me back to the home office in Philadelphia, Pennsylvania, and offered me the sales management position of the specialty products for the western United States. We wrestled with this for a little while and decided to take it.

My office was at the South San Francisco Airport. Our home in La Crescenta sold quickly, and we bought twenty acres in Calaveras County, at Burson, about thirty miles east of Stockton. We designed a home to build on the twenty acres and in the meantime set the Airstream trailer on site. There was already a well and power there. It was fenced in with another twenty acres, and we had free rein on it all. Forty acres with all our horses in our backyard. It was 120 miles from our home to my office. Of course, it was not a daily commute. I would go in on Monday, spend the day in the office, then fly out distant points, come back Friday spend a little time in the office, then drive home. I was back in the same mode as when I was with All American.

Dawn started her first year of high school in San Andreas, the county seat of Calaveras County. With winter coming on, we felt it wasn't good to spend it in the Airstream, so we rented a home in Valley Springs a few miles closer to San Andreas. Coming home one weekend, Nana showed me an article in the paper with some drawings of a planned freeway that would go right through our twenty acres. Again we began to talk about me finding work where I would be at home. We even bought a few beef cows and could pasture them with our horses. I think we bought ten. We were again getting serious about making a major change and even considering purchasing a ranch far away from the cities.

I came home a little later, and Nana told me she had found an interesting article in the "Farmers Home Journal" that we had subscribed to for many years. It was a story of a farm couple that had developed their farming operation into a guest ranch for boys and girls. That was it, the decision was made. I would resign, and we would search for an ideal location to develop a similar plan. We would stay in the West, however. The story was part of a farming operation in the East. The search was on.

It was a year or two before this that Danny had refused to go back to Gem State. He was home and would not go to school, said he would get a job and pay for his life at home. We had a pickup, and he wanted to buy it. So, in an effort to teach him some responsibility, I took him to the bank and signed a note, and the bank loaned him the money to buy the pickup. The result was that I made every payment. He wanted to join the Marines, and as much as Nana and I tried to change his mind, we finally signed for his enlistment and hoped that the training there would give a positive base to his life. During the time of his enlistment, we had moved to Valley Springs, spent considerable traveling in search of an ideal location to begin the development of our new idea. Dawn had been enthusiastic about every place we looked at.

There was one rather unique place we looked at out of Hood River, Oregon. It had a private road about ten miles in length that led into an attractive cabin in a beautiful setting with an unlimited view. There in the front of the cabin were a couple of elk. The privacy was unbounded with no neighbors for perhaps ten miles. It looked good, but we had to decline because of the concern that should medical attention be needed for our guests, the distance would be unreasonable.

There were some criteria that we felt should be given top consideration. One would be reasonable access to air transportation from the ranch site, and that the air terminal was serviced well from distant locations. I had used air service into and out of Boise, Idaho, some and was impressed with the fact that parents could place their child on a flight from almost any major location in the US and either have a direct flight into Boise or would necessitate not more than one flight change.

Next, we planned an investigating trip to Idaho. We looked at a few possibilities in Garden Valley, then had a meeting with Sterling Alley. He directed us to a ranch on the highway of 250 acres that had about a half-mile frontage on the beautiful South Fork of the Payette River. There was a large barn but no house or other buildings. The barn set nearly a half mile off the highway on a rutty dirt road. The owner lived across the highway in a manufactured home on a few acres that he was unwilling to include with the ranch.

It was a rainy, cold day when we looked at the property and Earl Simpson, the owner, offered to take us to the barn and that part of the ranch with his old John Deere tractor and hay wagon. Nana declined to make the journey, so she stayed in the car parked along the highway while I rode back with him. The view overlooking the river was spectacular, except that there was an area that Simpson had permitted the community to deposit their trash. I reported to Nana that the home we had designed for Burson should be planted right here in Garden Valley overlooking that pristine river in this little valley surrounded by magnificent mountains.

The next trip the weather was good, the road could be handled by our car, and the decision was made. We bought the ranch, named it Garden Valley Ranch, and began to put together the operating plans for our cattle operation and youth guest ranch. We also purchased from Simpson fifty head of cattle and the Forest Service grazing permits. As this plan continued to take shape and come together into a long-range operation, I am sure that the reader of this history will agree that God's hand was in it from the very start and that it was He that had led us to where we are.

The decision was made, and the deal was put together in the fall of 1968; by spring we had the plan pretty well in focus. I came to GV and got things underway. Nana and Dawn would stay in Valley Springs until Dawn finished the school year. We would then bring our horses, cattle, dog, and Airstream and begin life in a totally different world. Our furniture was already in storage. Danny was in the Marines.

While living in the Burson-Valley Springs area, we became friends with a couple who raised Arabian horses. By the time we left the area, we had come to visualize the value of the Arabian breed. We purchased two Arab yearling foals, one a chestnut stallion named Ali Sarie and the other a grey filly we called Missy. In my years of experience with horses, I have come to respect and love this breed. I am convinced that crossbred foals from other breeds make the ideal horse to be used in the outfitting business in dealing with people. They are smart, easy to train, they seem to like people, and they carry the same load as the larger breeds with a noticeably greater endurance. Over the course of the years, we owned three stallions and raised from fifteen to twenty foals almost every year. I had many favorite horses, but the best was a three-quarter Arab black mare with four white stockings named Snow Flake for that emblem located between her eyes. How I wish she were still alive.

My education involved becoming acquainted with flood irrigation, which we, within a few years, changed to sprinklers on the 100 acres of the irrigated part of the ranch. The cattle were part of what was known as The Garden Valley Allotment on USFS land in Bear Valley. There were nearly 500 head that were included in that allotment and in late spring were brought together and driven the sixty-five miles into Bear Valley and onto the allotment for the summer. A neighbor by the name of Harry Youren had 256 permits on this allotment, and he wanted to sell. He wintered his cattle in Horseshoe Bend, and after some investigation, we decided to purchase his cattle and USFS permits. This gave us a little over 300 permits. The cattle we were bringing up from California would not be permitted on the permit and would have to summer on the ranch.

The drive to summer range covers about sixty-five miles and would leave Garden Valley about the 25th or 26th of June. The cattle were put together in Garden Valley. The first day put them in Danskin, about ten miles along the way. Since the calves were young and the road traveled was still gravel, the next day they were given to range on the open hillsides above the river. The third day, early in the morning they were gathered and started on the trail again, much of this day's drive up some steep grade and by noon or shortly after were at a campsite on Big Pine Creek.

Joe Webster from Horseshoe Bend who was a permittee on the GV allotment with about a hundred head had an old bus that they had made a feeble attempt to fashion in it a kitchen and it was used to feed those who were driving the cattle. Iva, Joe's wife, was in charge of food service, and Nana was along to help and learn the procedures. But now that all the participants are dead, I can relate that Nana was unable to ingest the food. She had decided that some changes would have to be made in the food service department that would make the food palatable for human consumption. And believe me she did, and she did it diplomatically. Iva and all the crew, in the years to come, applauded Nana's culinary abilities plus her cheerful out-going personality.

While on the subject of food service allow me to stay with it and describe how the change and progress developed. By the next season we had installed a modern gas-fired kitchen in Daddy's Ditty Service. Through the summer guest ranch season, we had it backed up to a 16×24-foot squad tent with picnic tables where our guests were served first-class dining. During the cattle drive, it was driven along and continued to have first-class dining. To replace the service of the Ditty Service, we had purchased a two-ton International truck in which we could haul ten head of horses.

Back to the cattle drive: From Big Pine we would move the cattle up to the big bend in the creek, which had only limited space for the night's camp. But the cattle were pushed some beyond the camp up a very steep shortcut through the timber. Then the next morning that country was ridden again to gather any strays. That put us to the top of Scott Mountain, an elevation of 8,600 feet. There was a steep decent going down to Scott Creek, then up another short grade and into the drainage of Nine Mile Creek. There was a very nice roomy site along the creek.

The following day we came to the lake on the Deadwood River. We would cross the river below the dam and travel up on the east side of the lake to Bummer Creek. That was our camp with only one more day left to get on the allotment. The next year we changed the campsite to a large area on the side of the lake. Out of the Bummer Creek camp, we would drive up an old Jeep road, past the Mary Jane and Mary Blue mines, past the Pine Flat Campgrounds, over the summit into Bear Valley. Just as a matter of interest, Bear Valley Creek and Elk Creek are tributaries to the Middle Fork of the Salmon River. To that point all the drainages were contributory to the Payette River system.

That pretty well puts into focus the route and action involved with the cattle drive. Some changes were made by us as the years went by. One change of interest we made the following year, was to take some paying guests on the drive. This proved to be a good move, and some of the guests enjoyed riding along on horseback with the privilege of yelling at the cattle so much that they would come back additional years. One time I went into the bank we used in Cascade, and the owner of the bank who had turned out to be a good friend, Frank Callender, called me into his office. He said, "Dan, you're the first person I ever knew that got people to pay you for helping you drive your cattle."

One year we had a professional photographer whom we had met at a sports show in California and who rubbed shoulders with all the Hollywood people, who wanted to come and photograph the drive. He did, but in the end, I don't know whatever became of the film. On one of our trips to a sports show down there he had us to a dinner with Lawrence Welk, and we had an interesting visit with him; also met some other personalities.

It must have been in the mid-seventies, sometime when long hair was a badge of attention among the hippy culture. We had a young fellow with long hair, late teens or maybe early twenties, that worked for us at the ranch. I can't remember his name. He wanted to go on the cattle drive with us, but I told him that his long hair would not be accepted by the cowboys or the guests. Then I suggested that we would include him in the drive as one of the cowboys if he would consent to our stringing him up by his heels on a tree limb and we would cut his hair. I told him we would make a movie of the action and he would be the star of the show. He thought about it for a few days and agreed.

The whole performance turned out pretty good. Glen Gussie, a well-known cowboy in the area, went through the process of roping him as he would a calf and threw the rope over a limb. After he was raised to where his head was a few feet above the ground, his long locks were cut with a sharp knife, and when back on his feet he did indeed look more like a cowboy. He had treasured his long hair more than he thought he would, and as a result, he did, for a short time shed a few tears. But he did turn out to be a good sport.

That was the year that Bob Plunkett, a professional photographer, was filming *History's Last Cattle Drive*. But we never got to see it on the screen. It must have been that year, though I am having difficulty trying to keep in focus what happened on what year, that we had planned, the night we camped on Big Pine Creek, for some professional western entertainment. Tom Carter who had some amplifying and other musical equipment, and was himself, and still is, a talented man before the microphone, provided some good songs with background music away up there on the mountain. Additionally, the Ridinhouer Sisters from Baker City, Oregon, and Carol Patterson all added a real dimension of the western atmosphere for our guests and the staff.

The youth guest operation was a fun way to earn an income. So many memories. Sometimes I wish we had kept in touch with those kids and found out what happened in their lives as they grew into adulthood. I remember a little slip of a girl by the name of Suzie. She may have been eight years old, because that was the bottom age limit we had set, but we may have been guilty of letting someone a little younger be a part of our group. She was from Salt Lake City, her father was a dentist or an MD, can't remember which. She had never been around horses, but she fell in love right away, and at the end of two weeks when her parents came to get her, she demonstrated how she could get on the back of a fifteen-hand horse from the ground, the horse being bareback, with just the strength in her hands and arms and the horse's mane. Then she'd ride bareback through the meadow with her ponytail flying behind her.

One great show of entertainment was a bucking pony we had. Dawn would lead this pony (it was much bigger than Shetland pony) to an area where there was some loose sand. The kids would get in line; Dawn would take them one at a time, help them to climb on to the bare-backed pony, and then lead it through the sand patch. The pony would buck the kid off, and then he or she would get up and go right to the back of the line again. One time there were two sets of parents from California who had come to pick up their children. They so enjoyed the whole show. Both of the fathers were large football players, and Dawn asked one of them if he wanted to be bucked off. He was certain that that little equine would not be able to buck him off, so he got on, and Dawn led him away. Though his feet almost touched the ground, the pony landed him in the sand patch. It was a pretty warm day, and his face that had come in contact with the sand was almost black. But he and all the rest were laughing and had enjoyed the whole show.

Deadwood Outfitters

The South Fork of the Payette had not yet been classified for float boating, but a year or two later when it was, we were given a grandfather's right and licensed with the state for commercial use. We had purchased a couple of rafts, and one day every week we would provide some whitewater fun for the kids. We would also on a day now and then load the kids up and take them on a sightseeing tour of Bear Valley when the big salmon were spawning.

Early in 1969, we purchased the outfitting business from Sterling Alley. So not only were we getting started in the cattle business and with a brand-new youth guest operation, besides building a new home overlooking the river, we also had the challenge of dealing with the hunting guests and the season coming up the middle of September. I did have the advantage of having personally hunted some of the very large hunting area, about fifty miles square. I had a couple of guides that had worked for Alley, and they had agreed to stay with me for the first season. Web Appel had died, and Frank Callender and four other men had purchased the old town of Deadwood from his widow. Nana would be there to do the cooking. Fortunately, most of the guests that first year were booked in as spike hunters, so there was only a few who were to be guided. The rest would be packed into and out of camps that we had already set up. That kept us very busy with long, long days and short nights.

By the first part of November, it was necessary to move out of Deadwood because of the buildup of the snow. To get out, we had to move the equipment over several summits. But the season then continued into the first part of December. From Garden Valley we moved a camp into Granite Basin which remained open until the end of the season. We could only accommodate a couple of hunting parties from that camp. We had packed out all the hunters and their camps that had to be reached from the Dead-wood base camp but had one on Lorenzo Creek that could be reached from the lower end up the Deadwood river from near Lowman. Trouble was I had never been into that camp from this access, but I made it.

The country to be hunted out of Granite Basin, which was and is an interesting country. Most of it good horse country and a good volume of both deer and elk. We were winding up the hunt and moving out. It was about twelve miles down to the ranch. So the tents and equipment were loaded on pickups, and I trailed the horses out. The only thing left was the party and camp on Lorenzo Creek.

We had packed the camp in from the upper Deadwood side while we still were operating out of the base camp, now the effort would have to be reached from the lower end of the river. The Deadwood joins the South Fork of the Payette a few miles downriver from Lowman, perhaps fifteen miles east of Garden Valley. From that point years ago the USFS had built a road seven miles up the Deadwood, with the intent of extending it all the way and connecting it with the road by the Deadwood Dam. After hav-ing built the seven miles, including a good bridge across the river, it was decided that it would be too expensive to follow the original plan. So the seven miles and the bridge, representing a couple of million dollars was thrown up, and the road was never maintained.

But at the time of this story, the road was still passable, as was the bridge. So, early in the morning, I loaded up four saddle horses for the guests, four pack horses for the camp, plus my saddle horse and headed up to the end of the road. Alley had given me a verbal description of how to reach the camp. The trail to reach the Deadwood trail was known as Daisy Creek Trail, and was a very steep switch-back trail up out of the river. From there I believe it was about seven miles to the Lorenzo camp. There was about a foot of snow on the ground and snowing at a pretty good clip. When I reached the camp I was informed that they had a buck, so the hunter that took him went with me to get it. By the time we got back to the camp it was late in the afternoon, and by the time we had the camp loaded, it was turning dark. One horse that had been a part of the purchase of the business, and which had no doubt been a good pack horse, now was dealing with a problem that would cause him to suddenly stop and plant his feet. With this action he would break the break-away, and I would have to stop and get him in the string again. The horse's name was Sox. The four guests were behind the pack horses, and by now it was totally dark and continuing to snow. About the third time Sox broke the break-away, he lost his balance and rolled down a steep slope along the trail. He rolled perhaps a hundred feet and landed against a windfall on his back. With the help of the hunters, working with flashlights, we were able to get to the straps and ropes and take the pack apart. Got Sox back up on his feet, and he seemed to not have any serious injuries. I led him back up to the trail, carried all of his pack up, and repacked Ol' Sox. Then we went on our way again.

Purposely I did not tell the hunters of the steep switchback part of the trail yet to come. But before starting down, I went back and checked all the packs with my flashlight and made sure all the saddle horses' saddles were cinched up tight. It was dark, and it was steep, but my faithful old Ringo horse led us down, and soon we were taking everything apart at the truck. It had what was called a large bang-board, a platform that was over the cab. We loaded the horses, but I cannot remember how we ever got all five of us in the cab of that old International truck. But we must have accomplished it somehow. We made it back to the ranch where their vehicles were, and I do remember the good friendship that developed out of that experience. They came back and hunted with us again. Remember, this was my first year with the business. No question in my mind that God was leading in this experience and has continued to lead Nana and me throughout our lives.

During the winter we worked at finishing the home. We were living in the kitchen, two bedrooms, and the bath for a while, and had shut off the

> *I cannot remember how we ever got all five of us in the cab of that old International truck.*

living room, the master bedroom, and the other bath. Margie stained the tongue-and-grooved 1" × 6" lumber for the vaulted ceiling in the living room, and I put them in place. We were the butt of some criticism and displayed a degree of stupidity for building our home so far off the highway. Tradition demanded that residences be built by the highway so you could better hear the traffic or for whatever other reasons there may have been. Interestingly, as time has drifted by so many others have followed our decision. One thing for sure, the view from our living room window of the river and the mountain beyond has been of so much personal value to all of us.

Well, the die was cast; the transition from the previous lifestyle seems to have been complete, and only memories remained of Pennsylvania, California, and Japan. To be sure, there remained family, friendships, and contacts, but we were now winding up our first year in the cattle business, the youth guest business, and the outfitting business, and Idaho was our home. I remembered my first trip through Northern Idaho while hitching hiking from my discharge in California to the family home in Wattsburg, Pennsylvania and the impression Idaho made on my mind of its beauty, of the mountains, and the solitude. I had made the statement to myself that someday I would be back. Here I was, and I brought with me a wonderful and willing wife and daughter. Our older daughter, Carolyn, and her husband Art would be following us from California within a year or two, as would son Danny when discharged from the Marines. Here are some pictures of Danny's family. (81, 70, 71, 72, 73, 74, 75, 77)

Soon after our move from Pennsylvania to California, I approached Alan Fisher about the prospect of Ace Drill Bushing Company hiring Art. Alan said he had just the need for someone like him, and so Carolyn and Art moved to La Sierra. Now they would be making another move from there to Garden Valley. This move of theirs to Garden Valley was providential. Nana and I had decided to develop the 100 acres behind the Catholic Church and the public high school into one-acre lots. We planned to make it the first development in Boise County with a central water system and buried power and phone service. Arthur, with his background in building and construction, was just who I needed to head that work up. After that was getting pretty well along, we took on a franchise for log homes. I believe that we sold twenty log homes in a little over a year, and Art supervised nearly all of their construction. He and Carolyn were an important part of our activities in Garden Valley. Arthur passed away some years ago, but Carolyn is still a resident of GV and is retired after spending the last twenty years or so aiding in the food service of Camp Ida-Heaven in McCall, the Idaho Conference camp.

We wintered our cattle in Garden Valley and calved them out in February and March in two and three feet of snow. That may not seem to be a great achievement if only working with a few cattle, but with several hundred head, it did indeed become a major effort, requiring night and day attention. The next summer we purchased a sixteen-hundred-acre ranch near Sweet, Idaho, not far from Emmett and about thirty-five road miles from Garden Valley. That area gets very little snow and much milder winters than GV. There were no irrigated fields on the ranch, but it had a nice comfortable home and a barn in good condition. After trailing the cattle out of Bear Valley in October, we would keep them in GV until we used up the feed we had there, then we'd walk them to Sweet for the rest of the winter and calve them there. In May we'd walk them back to GV with their calves, then on into Bear Valley for summer range in June. In trailing them between the ranches, we had to go down the highway to and from Banks, where we crossed the river and used gravel roads through Dry Buck and on into Sweet again on paved roads through the little village and on up to the ranch. It worked out quite well.

It was fairly common when a group would come into our camp for a summer pack trip into a backcountry lake or for an elk hunt in the fall, that one or more of the party would come to me and make it known that they either had never ridden a horse or did not have much experience and ask that we be sure to give them a gentle horse.

Our standard response was, "don't be the least bit concerned, we have all kinds of horses, we have tall horses for tall people, short horses for short people, fat horses for fat people, skinny horses for skinny people, and for people that have never ridden we have horses that have never been rode!"

Tragedy Strikes

One very emotional story that needs to be a part of this historical study, Dawn, who was so personally involved, has to write. She is the only other person still alive who has first-hand knowledge of the tragedy, plus a more accurate memory of its development than I.

This written by Dawn Carter:

Dad has asked me to tell this story. It is something that had an indelible mark not only on me as a teenager but on Dad and Mom as well. To give a little back story, when we moved to Idaho, the plan was for me to go to Gem State Academy as a tenth-grade boarding student. I was not overly keen on the idea, as I loved the ranch and wanted to be there. The fact, too, was that I was extremely shy and did not relish going to a new school (and living there!) when I did not know a single person there. It was tough for me, and the roommate I was assigned was less than helpful!

After a while, I made friends with another ranch girl, Cheri Barker, from Bellevue, Idaho. Her parents had a sheep ranch that had been in their family for generations. We hit it off and had a great time together. I loved visiting with her parents and family on their ranch, and she so enjoyed mine. School did not seem so bad. We finished out our sophomore year well and had great plans for our junior year. That year also was a good year. We were as close as many sisters, both of us being the youngest in our families with older siblings already gone from the home.

Great plans were laid for our senior year and beyond. Cheri had wanted for the longest time to get her parents and mine together and for them to see Deadwood, so after much cajoling and working hard to get their hay crop in, she convinced her folks to meet me and my parents at Deadwood for a weekend. We had such a good time, and it was fun to see our parents enjoy each other as they did. It was the week before school started, and it was a hot August day. We had ridden horses for a *long* time. Probably at least ten miles or so, and we were hot and sweaty, so we decided to go down to the lake for a swim. We took John with us. He was a boy of fourteen years, I think, that had spent most of the summer with us. We had a great time; the water was perfect. Cheri and I swam for a while. John hung out on shore.

We were right at the top end of the lake where the river runs in, so the river channel is there on the right side, but where the lake spreads out to the left, it goes out for a long way, has a grassy bottom, and is pretty shallow. We had gone out there a long way and were just over our heads swimming when Cheri—the distance runner/athlete—had a strange look and said, "I am tired, I can't swim anymore." So I said, "Okay, let's go back." And she replied, "I can't." I told her I would pull her back. I remembered the rescue hold and started to swim with her. Somehow, I think we had gotten off into the river channel. It seems as though I swam for a long time and I was getting tired. I asked her to kick to help me, but she did not respond. John saw us from the shore, and he ran to the campground nearby for help. There was a church group camped there, and this guy just came flying toward us kicking off his shoes, his hat, and shirt and yelled at me, "Are you in trouble??"

By this time I had gone under a couple of times trying to hold Cheri up. The guy swam out to me and grabbed Cheri from me and pushed me toward shore. He told me he had her and for me to get out. By this time we were very close to the shore. It took me only a moment to reach the shore. When I turned around, the man was about in the same place I had left him but without Cheri. He dove for her several times but could not find her. He said that when he took her from me, he asked her if she was okay. She reached up and wiped the water from her face and shook her head yes. He swam only a couple strokes when she grimaced and put her hands and feet against him, pushed away, and sank out of sight. I kind of fell apart. A big heavyset lady from the church group wrapped a blanket around me and handed me a cup of coffee. I said, "Please, would someone go for our parents?" I gave directions to her, and she left.

Unbeknown to me at the time, John had left in our pickup for help. He was only fourteen or fifteen and had just had a few driving lessons from Dad that summer. Things were all kind of a blur for the next little while. I remember sitting on the bank wrapped in the blanket and just in a daze. After what seemed like forever, I heard a car pulling in very fast, and it drove right up to me. I could not look up. Dad and Cheri's mom, Evelyn, got to me first. The lady who went for them did not know our names or how to describe us, so the parents did not know which one of us was gone. I remember Dad lifting my face up in his hands, and he was crying.

Evelyn fell across my lap crying and hugging me and said, "Oh, Dawnie, I am so glad you are okay." Mom and Curt (Cheri's dad) were there then, too. It was a tough, tough scene. Curt walked out into the water and just stood there for a long while. Then we had another trauma to deal with. John had left in the pickup, but had not gotten to the camp, nor did they see him anyplace along the way. Oh my! Come to find out, when he had gotten to the forks in the road, he decided to drive to Elk Creek guard station and get help from the Forest Service. He was safe, and the guys from Elk Creek brought him back in good shape.

Losing Cheri was a huge blow to all of us, but it was so, so hard on her parents. They had become Christians when she was quite young, but her older brothers and sister were in high school, so none of them had taken hold of the faith. Cheri was the only one. She was very close to both her dad and mom, and she was so precious to them. Her parents became almost like second parents to me, and I loved them dearly. Such wonderful people, and I do still miss them. How to survive these kinds of trials without the hope in Jesus is unfathomable to me.

Cheri loved Jesus, and I do not doubt that I will see her again in heaven! I cannot wait to drag Tom up to her and say, "See, you were right! He did like me!" (Tom had flirted with me in school, and she had told me that he really liked me, but I had poo-pooed the idea! LOL!!), and to have her meet my kids and grandkids! She will love you all sooo much! She was such a fun person with a great sense of humor. Her parents never did have an autopsy done to find the cause of death. She did have terrible nosebleeds from time to time. She could fill the bottom of a wastebasket an inch or more with blood. I feel that she had some kind of an aneurysm or something in her brain and had experienced a stroke or something like that. I guess the details will not be known, but the surety of seeing her in heaven and spending eternity in friendship is very sure!

Now, this is turned back over to Dad:

I would like to pause in this narrative and offer a few thoughts of a spiritual nature. It is my belief that most things that occur or happen in our lives are not coincidental, just happening by coincidence. I believe that God has a direct interest in the lives of each individual. I don't believe that it is just a coincidence that you are reading this historical record of the family, nor that it was just a random effort on my part to put it together. For years some of my grandchildren have urged me to provide some record of their background. Danny's family has been very vocal, feeling perhaps that having been raised without much contact with the rest of the family they have developed an inert desire to have some knowledge of family history. For years, I kept promising that I would make the attempt, but always found something to interfere. My brother, Bud, passed away three years ago. Had I launched this effort before that, he would have offered a great deal of help. Still, I have my sister Janie and Bud's widow, Sweetie, and I hope they will be willing to contribute.

But behind it all, I have felt impressed that the tone of this document should concentrate on God's love for each of us and that I will be successful in directing attention to that goal. Because of conditions in this old world, I believe that Jesus will soon come and put an end to all the separation, heartache, hurt, and sin. The greatest longing of my heart is that I will spend eternity with the family I have here on this earth now. So my plea is that those who will read these lines will understand that the intent, on this old fellow's heart, is that all of us will, without the loss of a single one, be ready to meet Jesus.

Should there be any indication that the stories and incidents that I am recording suggest in your mind that I am calling attention to me, I hope to dispel that thought by stating that it is my belief that this old piece of clay has absolutely no inherent qualifications or abilities except as they are supplied by the almighty power of God. Even the effort that is going into this historical study, though requested by family members, has been acted on by me because of an impression coming from above. Anything that has been accomplished of value by Nana and me in the past, we have understood it to have been under God's direction and could not have been otherwise achieved.

Adventures and Misadventures

A rather interesting snowmobiling event occurred about the second or third year after we were authorized to build structures and offer a winter service to the public at the Deadwood camp. A somewhat disabled Vietnam veteran asked for the job of caretaking the camp during the winter. He was a very honest and upright gentleman and did a very good job. He was somewhat limited because he was unable to shovel the snow off the roofs and was very reluctant to operate a snowmobile.

We had agreed to watch the camp while he took a one-week leave midway through the winter. Nana wanted to go in and spend the week with me. We thought that would be a great vacation and time to spend some quiet time together. It was before we had built the private cabin, so the living quarters were in the southern end of the lodge building. The kitchen truck had been parked under cover beside the living quarters. The large round, open fireplace was in the center of the one-hundred-foot pole building, and the fifty-foot-long house trailer was under the same cover on the north end of the building. That trailer had five rooms in it that served as sleeping rooms for guests. Then beside the trailer and undercover, was wood storage that would accommodate about twenty cords of firewood.

Nana and I arrived on two snowmobiles in the middle of the day, and I took the caretaker on my machine and headed for Cascade. My cargo sled was attached with some emergency supplies. At that time the road was plowed about five miles to where the plows could turn around. That left a distance of about forty-five miles from the camp to where we could connect with the caretaker's brother who was to meet us.

We made it all right to a point of about one mile short of Landmark when the snow machine broke down. Still thirty miles short of our destination, we walked on into the old Landmark USFS station, where I broke into a cabin, built a fire, and left some food for my friend. Then I walked back to the broken-down equipment where I had my cross-country skis, put my backpack on, and started for Deadwood and Nana, fifteen miles away.

By the time I got to the Deadwood Summit, it was pitch dark. As always, I took my skis off when traveling downhill. I was headed down a three-mile steep grade at night. About a half mile down, the trail makes an "S" turn and crosses a little bridge (or culvert) over the upper reaches of the Deadwood River. I thought that I had missed that turn in the trail and was below it, so I turned to my right and started to climb the mountain, dragging my skies in the hopes of finding the trail. After considerable climbing I concluded that I had made a mistake, so I started back down at an angle. I found the trail and continued on, with still about four or five miles to go. Somewhere around two or three in the morning, there was the camp, just where I had left it. Nana had the light on and was happy to welcome me back. She fixed a good hot meal of pasta as I related my story. She told me she had radioed out and made a report to the sheriff's office.

Just as I started to eat, three searchers came in on their machines. They were most anxious to understand what it was that I was dragging behind me, and why I left the trail and started to climb the mountain. But they said that they were happy when they found where I had reentered the trail. Margie invited them for a meal, but they declined. Said there were a couple of others in their party, and they had taken the caretaker on to Cascade.

We had a five-year lease on the Mills' ranch that neighbored ours. We had turned cattle into that ranch across the fence from ours. I felt the need of another bull and wanted to try Black Angus for some crossbreeding. I bought a nice looking yearling from Goslin between Horseshoe Bend and Emmett, brought him home, and unloaded him at the barn. There was a gate in the fence about a quarter mile from the barn. I saddled Ali Sari, went out, opened the gate, came back, and hazed the bull along the fence line. When he came to the gate, he went right on past it, so I got ahead of him and turned him around. He went right on by it again and went back to the barn. I was trying to haze him back to the fence line again when he charged my saddle horse right behind his front legs and tipped him over on me.

I picked up my left leg and noticed that it did not bend at the knee, but above the knee. Had a young fellow working for me by the name of Billy Franklin. I told him there was a rifle in the pickup. If the bull charged again, to shoot it. I told him to take Ali Sari and tie him up in a stall in the barn, then go and ask Nana to bring the station wagon down. I told them that there was a sheet of three-quarter-inch plywood in the barn that they could use to get me on in place of a stretcher. Providentially, two men came down the driveway and helped load me into the station wagon. Interesting how things just seem to "happen," wouldn't you agree? Nana was going to take Billy along, but I said I would be OK, and he should stay at the ranch while she took me to Emmett.

It was a compound broken femur. About three inches of the bone had been shattered into bits and pieces. An orthopedic surgeon from Caldwell came over, and surgery was performed a week or so later. They had "just happened" to find in my pants a bone fragment, a sliver, about the length of the missing section. In x-rays you could see that sliver lying, not in a straight line, but catawampus, at kind of an angle. The surgeon told me that there was only a small chance that that fragment would carry blood, and if it did not, I would most likely lose my leg.

It did carry blood, and two or three weeks later, all the while in traction in the hospital, an x-ray showed the misty outline of a new bone. By the way, this surgeon's name was Wolfgang Kanuchule. He had been a German Luftwaffe pilot during the war and had shot down allied planes over the English Channel. He was shot down, taken prisoner, and sent to America. After the war he came back, studied medicine, and became an MD.

One day when the local doctor came in to visit before he left, I asked, "Why not let me go home? I can heal there just as well as here." He laughed and said, "If you can figure out a way to not change the weight in the traction for even a second, we will think about it." Then he started out the door. I said, "Wait a minute! I have it all figured out. I'll rent this bed from you, and we can get the help to load me in the back of a nice new thirty-foot trailer."

He said he would talk to Wolfgang. They decided it would be all right. So the trailer was brought to the ER entrance, and the doctors and everyone else got involved and seemed to have a lot of fun. The bed was secured to the floor, and Dawn sat there all the way to Garden Valley holding the weight over the bumpy road. They took me in the double doors and set me with a view of the river and the mountains, next to a glass sliding door where the hired men could come, and I could get involved in running the ranch. Two or three weeks later the procedure was reversed. Upon my arrival at the ER entrance, there was a sign over the door that said "WELCOME BACK COWBOY." I still have that same leg, and it still works. Once again, it is necessary to bring God into focus in this life history. The hospital director was Newton States, who has become a lifelong friend. He and his wife are members of the Emmett Seventh-day Adventist Church.

By late summer I was out of traction. With a cast on from my hip to my toes, we packed for an overnighter out of the ranch with our youth guest kids. Dawn and Nana helped me up on old gentle Suzie, tied my cast to the saddle horn, up along her neck. We spent the night up on the mountain with a good campfire and came back to the ranch the next day.

Winter Challenges

We had been offering winter service to snowmobilers as a result of an agreement between ourselves and the USFS. For several years we kept a caretaker in the camp and had put in a 500-gallon storage tank for gasoline. We could provide sleeping accommodations and serve meals to snowmobilers. We also had radio service to function as a weather station for the Weather Service and to handle emergencies.

One winter, perhaps in the late 70s, we were running low on gasoline. I made plans to haul two fifty-five-gallon barrels on a sled that I had used for the purpose of keeping the camp supplied with food and equipment. The Lowman District Ranger, Gene Brock, said he would like to go along. He brought another man, and we started out from Lowman. It is forty-five miles to the camp from Lowman traveling up Clear Creek and into Bear Valley. We went twelve miles up Clear Creek to the mouth of Horse Creek. But try as we would, we were unable to make it up the steep grade of Horse Creek and into Bear Valley, because of the depth of new snow. After several hours of trying to break trail up the steep grade, we had to turn around and head back to Lowman. After getting the snow machine and the barrels of gas loaded again on the trailer, I told Gene that I was going to attempt to make it in through Cascade and Warm Lake. I asked if he would like to go along with me. The answer was a firm NO. He said he had enough for one day and had to be at work early in the morning.

I drove back to Garden Valley, told Nana what my plans were, then drove the fifty miles to Cascade. From there it is fifty miles into camp, but the road was plowed for about five miles out of Cascade toward Warm Lake. There I unloaded, and with considerable effort, was able to load the two gas barrels onto the cargo sled. From there to Landmark (about nine miles beyond Warm Lake) the trail had been groomed, so for about thirty-five miles, I was to have a nice groomed trail. However, I had two summits to go over before getting to Landmark. The first summit was Big Creek. I was cruising along making good time, but my powerful machine reached its limit just a few hundred yards short of the top of the seven-thousand-foot summit. I wrestled one of the drums off the sled and was successful in getting to the top with the other one. I unloaded it, went back and loaded the other, then put the second one back on and headed down the grade. When reaching the Warm Lake Lodge, which was closed down for the winter, I was sure that I would not be able to make it up the steeper Warm Lake Summit with both barrels, so I unloaded one there and was on my way again.

At Landmark the groomer headed north on Johnson Creek to Yellow Pine, and I headed south to Deadwood. It was fifteen miles from Landmark to the camp. The trail wasn't groomed from there on. There had been snowmobiles over the trail, but it was not possible to exactly determine where they had traveled, because there was about eighteen inches of new snow. It was after one o'clock in the morning when I started on the ungroomed trail. There were no steep upgrades to deal with, but I was traveling through some open country where the trail was not obvious. Several times I'd get off to one side or the other, and the cargo sled would tip over on its side.

Somehow, I was able to get the sled set back up on both runners and be on my way. A barrel of gasoline weighs about 400 pounds. Soaking wet I weighed about 150. God is good, and I made it into camp just as the care-taker was recording the weather to call out the report. On my next trip in, I picked up the other barrel in Warm Lake.

It was several years later; I had purchased an older Thiokol Snow Cat. It had large tracks, a cab with a heater, windshield wipers, and a cargo space. On the trip out through Bear Valley, about ten miles from camp, it stopped dead in the middle of the trail. The motor ran, but the snowcat was dead. It was late at night, so I figured I would stay with it until close to morning. It was in the spring of the year, late April or early May. It was raining a pretty good clip, and though there was still an abundance of snow, there were places that the water ran with determination.

I had skis with me, fortunately, since the wet snow would make slogging through it pretty tough. My pickup and trailer were at the mouth of Horse Creek toward Lowman, about twenty-five miles from my breakdown. It was about twenty miles to Highway 21 and about six miles from my breakdown to the Elk Creek Station. So I decided to head for the highway after making a stop at the USFS station, where I hoped someone would pick me up and at least get me to a phone. I was soaking wet when I arrived at the guard station, so I found an open window in the main house, built a fire,

> *I was soaking wet when I arrived at the guard station, so I found an open window in the main house, built a fire, and hung my clothes up to dry, built a fire in the cook stove, and fixed something to eat.*

and hung my clothes up to dry, built a fire in the cook stove, and fixed something to eat. I put myself back together and started on the balance of fifteen miles to the highway.

About a third of the way I found that the road through Bruce Meadows was clear of snow. Carrying my skis along with my backpack, I made pretty good time, but then as soon as I crossed the Meadows, I was back into snow, and it kept getting deeper as I climbed up toward Fir Creek summit. Short of the top, I was getting pretty tired, so I stopped and made a little camp and fire. It had stopped raining, at least for the moment. I had a serving of hot soup and rested some. The going to the summit was pretty difficult, and it was dark when I reached the top. Always, because I am not a skier, I take my skis off and carry them down steep grades. This time, however, I found that the wet snow allowed me to ski, sinking in and using little effort going downhill.

It was around eleven o'clock when I got to the highway. I was pretty sure that there would be no vehicles all night. It was raining again, and I thought of building another fire. I leaned back against a snow bank, and every time I would begin to doze off, I would come awake thinking I heard a vehicle. Then the third time, it did indeed turn out to be such. It was dark, and I had no reflective clothing, so I stood to the side, leaned out, and waved my arm. He kept on going, then his brake lights came on, and he backed up. He was a USFS employee on his way to Sun Valley for some early morning meetings, but he offered to take me to my pickup which was about forty road miles away. I said, "Oh, no. Just let me ride with you to Stanley, and I'll get to a phone where I can call my wife, so she won't report me missing." I was sure she would do that the first thing in the morning. After all, what could be more humiliating for an outfitter, than to have a search party out looking for him? So he did. I called Nana. I was able to get a motel room, and again everything turned out good. After the roads opened, I went in with the trailer and brought out the snowcat.

It had to be at the end of hunting season, or near the end. The cattle were off the permit and on their way to Garden Valley. I got word that a neighbor who I had befriended, had some good cattle grazing on his ranch on the South Fork across from Danskin Station, about ten miles above Garden Valley. The cattle coming off Scott Mountain would go past Danskin, almost to Garden Valley then cross the bridge and turn back up river to Bob Halstrom's ranch.

It was an open fall, and around the first of November, Curt Barker called and said he had a great deal of grazing on three or four thousand acres at Huddle's Hole, which is located near Arco, Idaho. Said he hadn't used it for several years, and we could have it. So we brought the cattle home from Halstrum's, weaned the calves, and ordered trucks in to transport several hundred head of cattle to the Hole about two hundred miles away.

Now, this Hole is a most interesting piece of geography. There is no fence to contain cattle in this cylindrical, but completely around it is an ancient flow of volcanic rock that, because of its structure, does not permit cattle to cross. Curt had built a road over it and placed a gate. The cattle were unloaded and driven through the gate. Not only did Curt give us the feed, but he also moved in a covered sheep camp on wheels to accommodate our caretakers. This whole experience has some most interesting features.

One: Though there were several thousand acres of good feed, the Hole has no water source, making it necessary to haul the water in a tanker truck about seven miles from the Lost River. Use of the tanker truck also was a gift from Curt Barker. There were several large water tanks wherein the water was placed so the cattle could drink. In the early part of this challenge the weather was favorable, but as the winter progressed, and to be sure the winter does just that in that high desert country, it was not so favorable. When pumping the water into the tank truck at the river, as the temp continued to drop, it was necessary to chop through deeper and deeper accumulation of ice. Then after arriving at the dump site for the water in the Hole, we had to have LP gas tanks and a flamethrower to open the valve.

Two: It happened that the caretakers for this project were none other than a newly married young couple, Dawn and Tom Carter. They lived in the sheep camp, in a small but cozy honeymoon cabin with a small wood-fired heating and cooking stove.

As the winter continued to lay more snow on the ground and the feed was getting somewhat difficult for the cattle, we drove the cattle to a ranch about six or seven miles from the Hole and purchased hay from the rancher. The ranchers were also a young couple, and they offered accommodations for Dawn and Tom, so they were out of the sheep camp. The cattle wintered there until they were getting close to calving, at which time we sent the trucks in and had them shipped to our ranch at Sweet where we calved them out.

I must add this little additional part to the story. About halfway through their stay in the sheep camp, I went over to take their place for several days. They had given me a little ball of fur for Christmas that year. It was a 'rough' German Shepherd; I think that was its designation. I had named him Buddy, and he had long hair. A super intelligent dog, so easy to train. The first night in the sheep camp the temp dropped to twenty or thirty degrees below zero, and Buddy froze to the floor. It didn't take much effort to get him unattached from the floor, and it never happened again.

Buddy was a close friend until he died at around fifteen years old. Good memories. I will ask Dawn and Tom to enter a postscript to this story. I am sure they can relate some interesting incidents that I am not privy too.

This is Dawn chiming in. This was quite the experience! I was pregnant with our oldest child Becky, and what I most remember about this is—living in a sheep camp in -20+ degree weather is not for the faint of heart. Sometimes it warmed up to 1 degree above during the day! We had bought *good* Eddie Bauer down sleeping bags with our wedding money. They zipped together to make a king-sized bed so we would stay cozy at night, but the bunk we slept on had a low ceiling over it, and our breath would condensate on it and form little icicles overnight. In the morning Tom would get up and throw some coal in the cookstove and light it and then jump back into bed until it warmed up. As the air in the sheep camp warmed up, the icicles would melt and drip down on us.

I craved fresh fruit while being pregnant—*really* craved it. Living in the sheep camp, it was not too readily available. Evelyn Barker had wonderful tomatoes from her garden that she ripened in her attic through the winter, and she gave me some! They were *soooo* good, just like fresh from a summer garden. I would keep them and the oranges I bought at the store in the bottom of our sleeping bag at night to keep them from freezing. Yes, you become resourceful in such situations!

We had our blue heeler dog, Honas. He was the best! It was so, so cold that we had him sleep in the sheep camp and even let him lie at the foot of our bed. In the middle of the night, the cows would get to rubbing on the camp and wake us up, so Tom would slide open the window above the bed and throw Honas out to chase them off and then have to get up to let him back in. Good memories for sure!

Back to Dad's story:

It must have been the second or third year in the outfitting business that it started snowing with a determination about the middle of October. We had already packed out the spike camps and only had a party of four deluxe hunters. On the 20th we decided to get out of camp and do it in a hurry. The guest had a four-wheel drive pickup; we had ours and the International stock truck. We loaded all the equipment and personal things in the pickups, loaded ten head of horses in the stock truck, and with everything chained up, we headed out. Going up the first summit, the truck spun somewhat sideways of the road, and I was stuck with the back of the truck hanging over a creek with about a ten foot drop out of the tailgate location, which would, of course, make it impossible to unload the horses.

I was shoveling snow when Nana returned with our pickup. We had it chained up on all four tires. I hooked a chain to the pickup, Nana was successful in getting me started, and we kept going to the summit. Whew, that was a close one. We made it through Bear Valley and over the Horse Creek Summit and on home. After unloading, I told the hunters that I was going to head right in to the camp in the pickup and would have to trail the rest of the horses out. Two of them volunteered to go with me. It had continued to snow all the time we were gone and, there was even more snow down on the Deadwood river than in Bear Valley. We had to stop on several occasions and clean the snow out that had built up in front of the radiator, causing the motor to heat up.

Arriving at the camp, I asked the men to get a fire going in the lodge and get some food while I fed the horses and got them ready to go. They did, and I told them to head on out. I put saddles or deckers on the ten horses and headed out sometime after midnight. It was still snowing a pretty good clip. It was difficult for the horses to walk in the single tire tracks of the pickup. It must have been somewhat over halfway up to the Deer Creek Summit, that I put my saddle horse at the end of the string and took the second horse in the string as my saddle horse. It was daylight when I made it to the cow camp, where there was horse feed in the barn and people feed in the cabin. The cow camp in Bear Valley is about fifteen miles from the base camp on the Deadwood.

After about an hour, I put them back together and headed out again. It was dark again when I got down on Clear Creek, found a good place to tie the horses up, and some of the cowboys came out of Bear Valley where they had been looking for some strays. I arranged to get the stock truck brought up from the ranch and finished getting the horses home. Another experience that turned out successful because of God's providential hand in the affairs of this family.

Over the years there have been many horse wrecks that have taken a toll on this old body. One that keeps coming to mind happened on the Bull Creek trail, perhaps a mile above the Deadwood River, sometime in the late 1970s or early 1980s. I'd hired a new man and wanted to show him some of the trail system we used before hunting season started. We were also involved in training some colts for the trails. I gave the hired man a good solid trail-wise saddle horse, and I took one that had been ridden several times and showed good sense. I was halter-breaking another one. Along the trail the filly I was leading would occasionally haul back, and I would dally the rope on my saddle horn and pull her along. We got on a steep switchback section of the trail, and I had still had the rope on my saddle horn (bad mistake). She hauled back and turned my horse sideways to the trail.

I took the rope off the saddle horn and threw it on the ground, while my horse was trying to get her feet back under her. She went over backward on the steep grade, and it was nearly 100 yards before I stopped rolling. I did not lose consciousness but had the wind knocked out of me. My helper came over, and we talked a little. I was lying in the sun, and I asked him to take my legs and drag me over under a large tree a few yards away where it was closer to being level. I was wearing a down vest that was open, and as he dragged me, it bunched up into a cushion under my neck. Something was wrong with my arms, and the right one was uncomfortable. I asked that he help me to lay it up on my chest, then it kept slipping back on the downhill side. My horse had just moved a few feet away, apparently unhurt, and stood there. I told him there was some cord in my saddle bags and asked him to get it and tie my hand and arm so it would stay on my chest.

Then I asked him to ride back down to the camp and get one of the folding military cots we had and stop anyone that came by on the road and see if they would come up and help pack me out. I keep referring to how God has in His own way worked things out. Was it a coincidence that almost immediately a pickup came by with three men in it and one of them was a trained medic? They came up where I was, and I asked if they would get me down to the road and load me in the back of my pickup so I could get into Cascade.

We got down to a sizeable clearing at the river level, where my new medic friend ordered the hired man to go to camp and get on the radio and call for Life Flight. There was no use for me to argue. He was in charge, although I didn't think I was that seriously hurt. He told me that he had no doubt that I had a broken neck. The helicopter made it in, and I wound up in St. Al's Hospital in Boise. The results of x-rays proved a broken neck, fifteen fractures in my rib cage, and a smashed pelvis. Amazingly, I healed pretty fast and was able to deal with the season as a manager, but there wasn't much action on my part that season.

Nana

Nana has always been such an outstanding wife and helpmate for me. The years on the farm in Pennsylvania, she was always just as steady and cooperative as could be hoped for. When finances became tight, and they did become very tight, she never complained nor did we ever have fights or disagreements over money, or the lack thereof. When it became necessary for me to travel and be gone extended periods of time, and she and the children were left alone with no neighbors closer than a mile away, her attitude was

Our telephone hung on the wall and was a party line. The telephone company central office was in Wattsburg, and all calls, except a party line call, had to go through central.

constant. Always glad to see me when I came home. She would give me reports of how she and the kids would spend their time. She always raised a good garden in season.

Our telephone hung on the wall and was a party line. The telephone company central office was in Wattsburg, and all calls, except a party line call, had to go through central. It was under the management of a man named Kent who had had polio, but he had some operators that worked on schedules. One operator was Helen Hoag, George Hoag's wife. One day Sweetie's mother called central and asked Helen to ring Nana. Helen told Mrs. Krause that there would be no need to ring her because she was taking a bath. Helen said that she had just connected her with "so-and-so" and before they hung up Margie (Nana) said she was going to take a bath. Interesting lifestyle, would you not agree?

Every day I would call home, which was always from an outside phone booth, where the temp was always 100 degrees above zero, or twenty degrees below zero, or so it seemed. I would dial "0" and give the operator the number "17J," then would be told to deposit a given amount of money, for three minutes. That was the mode of communication then. No one ever thought of such a contraption as a cell phone.

When we made the move to California and the big city, WOW, what a change. There she demonstrated the classic lady that she always was. She took the responsibility for the children's education and always maintained a perfect home. Then some years later, we were back in the country again, operating a sizable cattle ranch and active outfitter business. We had some guests that returned to hunt with us year after year. Several for as long as twenty years. I remember that some would say the only reason they returned so often was that of the good meals that Nana always put before them. She was a great partner. A wonderful person and my best friend. (19, 41, 69, 65, 66, 109, 110, 112)

We decided to sell the cattle and the permits in Bear Valley. My friend, Frank Callender, who owned Intermountain State Bank, was also a cattle rancher and had wanted for a long time to have grazing permits in Bear Valley. The price of cattle had been increasing for some little time, and I had hoped they would continue to. Frank met me at the Sweet ranch in the spring while we were calving. He made me a pretty good offer for all the cattle and the Bear Valley permits. But I was a little hesitant and told him that it looked like the price would continue to increase. I remember so well he looked me in the eye and said, "Dan, if you want to sell and you get a good offer, you should take it."

Well, I told him I would think about it and let him know. I didn't call him, and then the price of cattle began to drop. When the market had dropped about $100 a head less than his offer, I sold them and the permits to Frank. Which goes to prove once again my experience in the cattle business was always to buy when the market is strong and sell when it is weak.

Admittedly, not a good policy. We sold the ranch in Sweet. That turned out better since property values had increased considerably. This was all somewhere in the mid-eighties.

Now going back in time to about 1974, Nana and I decided to subdivide the 100 acres of hill property, that was part of the original Garden Valley ranch. We divided it into lot sizes of from one to four acres. We put together the first subdivision in the county that had buried power and telephone lines and a central water system. The timing was pretty good on that move, and it has turned out to be a very nice project.

We had a log home franchise for Model Log Homes that were manufactured in Gallatin Gateway, Montana, for about a year or more. Five of them were built on the subdivision. I think we sold fifteen or more during the time we had the franchise. Art and Carolyn had moved to Garden Valley from California, and Art took the management of building the homes. He also managed the building of the roads and burying the utilities on the subdivision.

Then we purchased two ranches that joined our ranch on the river. That totaled about 450 acres, and we added to it the fifty acres of Garden Valley Ranch property on the river. We had it engineered for a residential subdivision, and it was to feature an eighteen-hole golf course. We had it engineered and had a golf course architect and all the lots laid out. We built one of the log homes on the property for an office. Had the governor of Idaho and the lieutenant governor come to an intense opening ceremony, with the news media and photos of the dignitaries driving golf balls from the patio off our home into the river. Every indication was that it would go and be a success. Then the president of the United States kind of had arrangements made that interest rates would go from five or six percent to twenty-one or twenty-two percent. We had a loan approved from California for the three and a half million dollars needed to do the project. We turned the loan down, and the corporation was forced into bankruptcy. The landowners from which we had purchased the real estate on contract, which included the fifty acres from Garden Valley Ranch, were able to repossess the land, so they were not to suffer any loss. That was, of course, a major loss and disappointment. The loss shattered the bank account and some of our dreams, but not our faith. Thank the Lord for that.

As winter was getting old and spring drew into focus, most years it would be expedient to get into camp with supplies and encourage the winter caretakers, that yes, the road would soon be opened, and he or they could again find contact with the outside world. Most of those years, along toward the end of April and into May, the snow would be off the roads in places, but still very evident in other areas. This made it impossible to travel by either four-wheel drive vehicles or by snow machines. So I would trailer horses as far as possible, then pack a couple of horses with supplies and ride the remaining distance, which could be from ten to twenty-five miles.

This particular year Dawn wanted to ride with me. We were able to trailer horses to near the top of the Fir Creek summit, leaving about twenty-five miles through Bear Valley, some of which was bare and part of it still loaded with several feet of snow, on past the Elk Creek Ranger Station (closed of course for all the winter). By late afternoon we made it to Elk Creek and the cow camp. We put the horses in the barn at the cow camp and gave them a good feeding, then walked back a couple hundred yards to Elk Creek Ranger Station. The ranger's residence was locked, so I helped boost Dawn through an unlocked window. She opened the door, and we proceeded to get comfortable for the night. Built a fire, had a good dinner, and a good sleep.

In the morning we began to put the horses together. In putting the pack on one of the young horses, I was lifting up the pack from one side, and Dawn was positioning a rope from the other side when the horse spooked, and somehow Dawn's collar bone was fractured. She was in quite a bit of pain, but despite my recommendations that we abort the trip and ride back the fifteen miles or so to the trailer and go home, she insisted that she would be OK and that we should continue. It was about five miles to Deer Creek Summit, and by the time we made it that far, she agreed with my promptings, and decided that we should turn around. From that point

I could reach the camp with my hand-held radio. I explained to the care-taker what had happened. I told him that he could come up to the summit on his machine and right at the summit sign, we would cache the supplies. I went into great detail in telling him that my transmission on my hand-held radio would not be picked up by Nana at home, but his transmission from the base radio would be picked up by her. I made it as clear as possible in plain English that he was not to repeat what he had been told about Dawn's injury on his transmission.

Somehow my instructions went over his head, and he repeated that he was not to confirm my instructions because it would cause Nana to worry about the problem. So the cat was out of the bag, and nothing could be done about it. Dawn had an uncomfortable trip back over the miles to the trailer, then the forty miles home to Garden Valley, then the seventy miles or more to medical help. She is a tough lady.

Here are some pictures of Dawn and Tom and their children. (116, 114, 115, 106, 104, 105, 80)

Sometime after moving from the farm in Wattsburg where circum-stances regarding finances had always been in a negative vein, we decided to always pay our tithe first out of any increase received. So long as we adhered to that decision, we always had sufficient funds to handle our obligations. We did become careless a couple of times over the years and again learned that God means exactly what He says. "Bring ye all the tithes into the storehouse, that there may be meat in mine house, and prove me now herewith, saith the Lord of hosts, if I will not open you the windows of heaven, and pour you out a blessing, that there shall not be room enough to receive it" (Mal. 3:10). When we erred, we would lose the blessing. Now I can testify after years of complying that the promise that the blessing is sure. I would strongly urge all my family to come to an understanding of this principle and test it out for yourselves.

We were successful in negotiations with the Federal Land Bank (or was it Farmers Home Administration, I can't remember), to satisfy the balance of our loan, by deeding the fifty-three acres on the river bottom to them, in exchange for their giving us a deed to our home, barn, and other buildings, and the irrigated land of the original ranch. Approximately 100 acres would be involved, and the deed provided us would be free and clear of any debt. Also, they would give us the right of first refusal for any sale of the fifty-three acres that may develop.

All things considered, this whole plan had to be structured under the direction of heavenly agencies, and there was no doubt that there was a purpose that God had in mind. Looking at it from any logical point of view, this business and financial agreement makes absolutely no sense.

Nana and I discussed this at great length. We had always had a desire to provide some benefit for children and young people, hence the established effort in behalf of the youth years before. I guess that we must have discussed this at some length with Dawn and Carolyn because Dawn put us in touch with Tom Sanford of Project Patch, and so was born a relationship that has developed into a most unique service to our fellow men.

After becoming acquainted with Tom and Bonnie Sanford and the impressive project they had only a few years before started in an organized effort to aid troubled teenaged boys and girls find a way back into society and build a beneficial future for themselves, Nana and I began to consider how we could best contribute to this worthy project. We prayed, we talked with Carolyn, Dawn, and Danny and others about how Garden Valley Ranch could perhaps be a part of this worthy goal.

The Idaho Conference and the North Pacific Union Conference of Seventh-day Adventist were brought into the discussion. Different ideas and plans were discussed over a period of time. Then Leon Cornforth presented a plan that seemed to fit the circumstances. His idea was that the gift of the ranch would be conditioned by giving Nana and me a life estate on the home and the ranch operation with the buildings and the 100 acres of arable land. We would execute our position to purchase the fifty-three acres on the river, and Project Patch would provide the money. The fifty-three acres would be deeded to Patch without any reserve of the life estate, and it would be the location for their operation. The plan seemed to be acceptable to everyone involved and was subsequently put into operation in 1989, and it became an operational reality in 1990. Soon it was taking shape. Construction of the dormitories and the core building that would provide kitchen, dining, and assembly space, and office accommodations. A dedication ceremony was planned, and before long the boys and girls were arriving. (55, 43, 63, 64)

As it took shape, Nana was asked to come and spend time in the girls' dorm through the evening and night hours. She developed a closeness with the girls and could better understand the importance and the need for Project Patch. (98)

There was a time during the 1990s and early 2000s, when Nana needed me to be close by, that I had the idea to build horse-drawn vehicles. So I bought some books on the subject and found some sources of supplies for the wheels and other components. I set up the workshop and started production building carts. It turned out to be somewhat successful and a great deal of fun. I remember training Snowflake, my favorite saddle horse, to work under harness. Some other horses also, but Snowflake most of all. She seemed to enjoy working with me on the project. I used her to travel to Crouch and on the highway to Garden Valley. One day I took Nana for a ride in the cart, and we went out to the highway, then down the Mills' driveway and back to Helen Mills' for a visit. Nana really enjoyed that trip.

I purchased a two-seated carriage with a fringe on the top from a man in Emmett that I had purchased hay from. When Bruce Biggs and Laurie from Patch were married by Tom Sanford there on the Patch front lawn, and I was asked to give the bride away, I hitched the big Shire team to the cart and carried the newlyweds up to the ranch house where they changed their clothes and left for the honeymoon. (86)

Patch was a very professional operation. They were very protective and careful to keep the boys and girls under the control and supervision of their staff. There was one young man, who no doubt because of his experiences, the staff seemed unable to reach into his life. I would be at a loss to explain in technical terms the problem they were having in trying to reach inside his heart and his mind, but for some reason, he did relate to the livestock, the horses, and the operation of the ranch.

The staff permitted him to come and spend a little time with me, and we developed a productive relationship in working together with the ranch chores.

As I understand Jimmy's (not his real name) background, he at the tender age of perhaps four or five had been present when his father had shot his mother and then shot himself. I think he was about thirteen or fourteen when he came to Patch, and he and I developed our friendship.

I don't remember if I had proposed directly to Tom Sanford, that I would be willing to take Jimmy on an overnight pack trip into the back-country and stay at the location of a hot spring. But, after some deliberation with the staff counselors, it was decided that it could be a good idea. So Jimmy and I enthusiastically began to make some plans. We would take two saddle horses and two pack horses, trailer them about fifteen miles up the Middle Fork of the Payette River to the end of the road. Then it was about another seven or eight miles to the hot springs. It's an interesting trip. The trail crosses the river on an average of about every mile. Then the hot springs are on a beautiful spot a little above the river with a good campsite and some grazing for the horses. It was a good trip, and we were back at the ranch the next afternoon.

Sometime later, Jimmy and I made another day trip on horseback. After that, I must have had to go back into the Deadwood camp and it may have been at the time that he graduated from Patch. I have lost track of him and time slips away. I must even now attempt to reestablish our friendship.

My Greatest Loss

The years slowly or rapidly, depending on your point of view, seemed to drift by and Nana's health was showing signs of slowing down by the end of the 1990s. But I am so very thankful that God made it possible for me to be with her through those years. God gave me good health; she never had to be put in a nursing home, which was of great concern to her. For some of those years, she could go with me to town when I had to do some shopping or take care of other business. We had to have an oxygen concentrator put into our home. For a while, she was able to ambulate with a walker; then she was confined to an electric wheelchair. I built some ramps so she could negotiate a couple of risers in the home. We were able to purchase a used van that I could put the wheelchair in, so she could continue to travel with me to town. By about 2003, Nana's health continued to cause more concern for us. We bought a travel trailer and took it on a couple of short trips close to home. One trip was to a campground on Hwy. 21 above Lowman toward Stanley. It was a very nice site and the weather, though a little cool, was good. The next day she was tired and wanted to return home. On another occasion we traveled to the Owyhee Reservoir south of Ontario. Another very nice campground and it was a good couple of days. The Newt States came and visited with us there one afternoon.

We had arranged to have Nana visit the Health and Wellness Center near Hermosa, South Dakota. The visit was to last two weeks, I think. She would be in a cabin. They permitted me to park the trailer outside the cabin where I could visit her a couple of times during the night because we did not include me in the program. She was in a wheelchair by that time, and I could stay with her in all the programs. I took my meals with her and the group but paid for the dining service.

Everything was just the way we hoped it would be, the service, the meals, the instruction in all the classes, and all the staff members were the right kind of people. About the middle of the second week, Nana became ill. The doctor on duty with the Wellness Center advised that she go into the hospital in Rapid City. There she got some better, but they advised that I should take her on home.

We left early in the morning, and by mid-afternoon she seemed to be losing contact with me. We had brought the oxygen concentrator along, and it was in the back of the pickup with a line from there into the trailer or into the cab of the pickup. But it had to have 120-volt power, which we had every night, but used a portable tank during the day. We were getting close to Dubious, Wyoming. We came to a trailer park near town, and I pulled in and parked in a good place. I had to help Nana to get into the trailer. Then I tried to hook up to power. But the camp was closed, and the power was shut off. I was getting very worried. I told Nana to just lie there on the bed, and I would drive into town with her in the trailer and find a place with power to hook up. I pulled into a motel and told them our problem, and he showed me where to park the trailer and hooked us up to power. In just a little while, she showed considerable improvement. After a good night's rest, we started on our way. Then about twenty miles out, she began to show signs of going into a coma. Pulling off the road, I took her oxygen off her face and found that there was none coming through the system. I went back into the trailer and got another section that goes into her nose, and that fixed the problem.

So without any other incident, we continued through Jackson Hole and on home. I took her to the clinic, and the indication was that had been the only problem. I wish that I had taken her to the Health and Wellness Center several years sooner. That is a good institution, and I believe that we could have added several years to her life had I made that kind of move.

I believe that the Garden Valley years have been covered up until we gifted the ranch to Project Patch in 1989 and 1990. It was around that time that we continued operating the outfitting business with the help of Dawn and Tom. Then in the mid-1990s, Nana began to have some more physical problems, and we turned the operation and the ownership of the outfitting business over to Dawn and Tom. They have since done a great deal to improve the operation, building a new lodge and barn and building and expanding the business. At this writing, they continue its operation. As the years passed, and Nana became more incapacitated, I was so pleased that I was able to spend more time with her and keep her at home. When son Danny passed away in 2003, she, Carolyn, Dawn, and I traveled in our van to his memorial in Meeteetse, Wyoming. It was a three-day journey, and she made the trip OK, except for all of us having to bid goodbye to our young son.

By 2006, Nana's condition had deteriorated to the point that Doctor Koenig put her in hospice care, and on June 18, 2006, we bid her farewell until the resurrection when Jesus shall return. She peacefully passed away in the home she had designed, and we had built along the river.

Project Patch offered the use of their facilities for a beautiful memorial service where more than 200 came to appreciate the service under the direction of Pastor Lyle Albrecht, on July 30, 2006. Dawn gave the eulogy, and Tom gave tribute with two beautiful songs. In the Patch Chapel, there was a continual showing of a beautiful DVD tribute to Nana, completely prepared by granddaughter Becky. A light meal was served, and good fellowship between family and friends was an important part of the day. The family and the world experienced a significant loss with the passing of this extraordinary lady.

You need to know that her mind and her attitude were always in excellent form. I read to her a massive volume of material. The Bible from cover to cover, all of the Conflict of the Ages Series, all of the Testimonies to the Church, Christ's Object Lessons, plus other books and articles. I must tell you without fear of contradiction, that those were the best years of our marriage. Still, up until her death, her mind remained clear and her attitude positive. I live in anticipation for Jesus to come when I can see her again.

We laid her to rest on a mountain ridge, and the spot is accessible by a two-hour ride on horseback. We have placed a plaque cemented into granite rock indicating her resting place and her hope to be awakened when Jesus comes. I try to visit the site every year. On a recent visit two very dear friends from John Day, Oregon, went with us. (103)

MY ANGEL (65)

God sent an angel to tame my soul
To be my wife, to make me whole.
As trials came, as come they may
She stood by me, be it night or day.
Thank You, Lord for the gift of my wife
Thank You, Lord for giving her life.
She made the road more easy to bear
She soothed my soul, with loving care.
Many the years she walked by my side
That dear angel I called my bride.
Lord, I know I didn't thank You enough
We forget you're there when times get rough.
Now that she's gone, O Lord, I pray
Help me to bear till that glorious day
When she shall awake, and I see her again
Please hold my hand, give me strength till then.
Written by Newton States—For his friend, Dan Rotthoff

But I would not have you to be ignorant, brethren, concerning them which are asleep, that ye sorrow not, even as others which have no hope. For if we believe that Jesus died and rose again, even so they also which sleep in Jesus will God bring with him. For this we say unto you by the word of the Lord, that we which are alive *and* remain unto the coming of the Lord shall not prevent them which are asleep. For the Lord himself shall descend from heaven with a shout, with the voice of the archangel, and with the trump of God: and the dead in Christ shall rise first: Then we which are alive *and* remain shall be caught up together with them in the clouds, to meet the Lord in the air: and so shall we ever be with the Lord (1 Thess. 4:13–17).

Life Goes On

After a short time of rattling around alone in our big house. I talked with Tom Sanford, and we made a deal for me to turn the life estate over to Patch. I bought a double-wide home and moved it onto a spot about a hundred yards from the home on Patch property. I lived there for over a year. Maranatha came in and overhauled our home into three apartments for Patch staff. It has made me so pleased to see the progress Patch has made in the lives of so many young people and continues to do so.

Then, in the declining years of my life, I was led to become a volunteer missionary pilot. I sold the double-wide to Patch for what I paid for it. I purchased a Cessna 182 airplane and got some refreshing flight instruction, since it had been a good many years since I had last piloted an airplane. Looking back, it is so interesting how God leads out in the affairs of my life. Here I was without a home to live in when I received an invitation to serve as a lay pastor in the small native fishing village of Togiak, Alaska. It had a brand-new parsonage for me to live in and work out of, in a field of endeavor I had no experience in.

Elder Ken Crawford, president of the Alaska Conference, gave me the invitation and was my mentor for the next four years. He and his wife Colleen became and remain good friends. They are now retired and have moved back to the Lower Forty-eight and have honored me with two visits to my humble home here in Ritter, Oregon.

The four years I served as a lay pastor in that far off land of Western Alaska in the small village of Togiak, on the shores of Bristol Bay, is an experience never to be forgotten. To be sure, it was a challenge of major proportions for this old man. You know that I was already in my eighties, which would indicate that I was already nearing the reasonable end of a long life. Why Ken Crawford gave me the invitation at that late stage in life, to tackle a challenge of such proportions, I don't know. But he did, and I am forever thankful. I traveled to give study to the invitation and also flew over to visit with the church and its people at Togiak. The church there had only been built a short time and was not completely finished. The parsonage was part of the church structure and not nearly finished. The pastor from Dillingham had flown me over and after a few days came back and picked me up in the Dillingham Church's Cessna plane. Then I traveled back to Anchorage on a commercial flight. While in Anchorage I met with the conference committee who questioned me at length, I guess to confirm and accept the president's decision to assign me to the responsibilities at Togiak. Then I went back to Idaho.

There is a story that needs to be told concerning the Cessna 182 that carried the (N) number—Two-Four-Niner-Niner-Golf, that I had purchased preparatory to my commitment to Alaska. The purchase had been made in June 2008 from the fixed base operator at the airport at American Falls, Idaho. After taking delivery, I spent the next few months getting updated on flying and using the plane to fly in and out of the back-country airports in central Idaho. Many of the back-country airports in Idaho are actually more of a challenge than are many bush country airports in Alaska.

When September came into focus and the time came for me to say goodbye to my established lifestyle in Idaho and to my many family and friends, and start a completely new way of life in Alaska, I was contacted by Ken Crawford, who advised that I should come without the airplane for the winter. He suggested that because of lack of airport security and hangar space in Togiak, I should come up and spend the winter, then go down in the spring to get the 182. He advised that the airport was at sea-level and the salt air would have a deteriorating effect on the aircraft frame. It seemed like good advice.

I had an old Chevy pickup, and I planned to drive it to Anchorage and leave it there. There are no roads connecting eastern Alaska to the western part of the state and Togiak was more than four hundred air miles from Anchorage. But when I was getting ready to leave, granddaughter Becky and her husband Bryon insisted that I take a more modern, and better-looking vehicle than that old rough pickup. They turned over to me a nice-looking SUV, and everything that I planned to take with me fit nicely into its cavity. So I loaded my things in it and headed for Anchorage. But this story deals with "Two-Four-Niner-Niner-Golf" and not with a road trip over the Alcan Highway, interesting as that trip was.

The winter showed up in Togiak along in November. Before long the bay froze over, and snowmobiles traveled on the ice extensively. It was a couple of miles across the bay to the Fish Cannery, and I was trying to stay in reasonable physical shape by walking every day. So on good days, I would take my exercise by "walking on water."

April showed up on the calendar, and I flew back to Idaho intent on bringing back the 182. I spent about a week flying around central Idaho and visited with family and friends. Since an annual would be due on the aircraft in June, I decided to have it done in Nampa, Idaho, rather than

> *I was trying to stay in reasonable physical shape by walking every day. So on good days, I would take my exercise by "walking on water."*

having it done in Dillingham, Alaska, where I did not have the contacts with any A&P's (Aircraft and Power Plant). The next day after putting it in the shop, the A&P called me and asked if I had had any hard nose wheel landings. I answered no. He said that it had had one or more and that there was between $25,000 & $30,000 damage on the airframe.

"The best-laid plans of mice and men!!!"

Was it a coincidence that a Boise attorney who hangered his airplane there at the Nampa Airport was present at the airport office at that time? As circumstances developed, I am sure it was not a coincidence. As usual, God had a hand in the circumstances.

The A&P introduced me to attorney Donald Lojek. Mr. Lojek had an airplane and kept it hangered there at the Nampa Airport. I had in my briefcase all the papers concerning the purchase of my Cessna 182, and after Attorney Lojek had taken the time to review them, he stated, "Dan, you would not stand a chance to recover anything from the seller because you had signed a document wherein you accepted the airplane as is. However," he said, "if there was an outside chance that fraud was involved and we could prove it, that could change." After some discussion, he agreed to take the case, and I gave him a small retainer to get things started. I flew commercial back to Togiak to take care of my responsibilities there.

Over the months that followed, Don Lojek and I communicated by phone and e-mail. He made several trips to American Falls, had numerous meetings with the defendant and his attorney and with possible witnesses. It must have been a year later that his efforts were successful, and the court awarded us a judgment to the extent of the full purchase price of the airplane, the attorney fees and all costs involved plus 5 percent interest. The court found the defendant guilty of fraud and his A&P, who had certified an annual inspection, lost his FAA licenses. Then Don Lojek notified me that the defendant had skipped out, and it had not been possible to serve him with the judgment.

When I received this news, I sent an e-mail to Don and asked him to supply me with the amount of his legal fees and an indication of what would be acceptable terms for me to pay the obligation. Seriously, I do not believe that it was more than fifteen minutes later that I received his e-mail in response, wherein he stated that he was impressed that I had made an effort to serve as a missionary to the natives in Alaska and that he was donating his fee. His fee represented more than $10,000. I am unable to find words to express the impression that this has had on me. I have truly been overwhelmed with gratitude and thanksgiving. Over the years that have followed Don and his wife, Cec, have become very close friends. Every time I am in the Boise area, they have invited me to dinner and have also made trips to come to my home here in far-off Ritter, Oregon. As I have grown older, I find that one of the most valuable assets of human life is the closeness of family and friends. Thank you, Don and Cec.

The conclusion of "Two-Four-Niner-Niner-Golf" is that Don came into contact with a man who has an airport near Mountain Home and is himself an A&P who wanted to purchase the plane. We agreed on a price of $15,000 for which I had paid $65,000.

I arrived in Anchorage in September and spent a little time being educated in what to expect as I became a part of the Yupik native culture. The church and the conference had bent every effort to have the parsonage finished when I arrived, and they had just about accomplished their goal. Only a little of the floor tile was left to do in the kitchen. Gavin Thompson came over from Dillingham and finished the job soon after I moved in. Dillingham lies across Bristol Bay to the east about an hour's flight by airplane.

Getting acquainted with the church members and the neighbors was an interesting assignment. Rumor has it that the natives usually do not readily accept newcomers, but I did not find that to be the case. They do however have a unique respect for the elderly, and my age may have been the reason that our friendship developed almost immediately. I want to introduce you to my friends there in Togiak, they who were not only friends there and then, but who have remained so over the years since my departure.

But first let me tell you about Togiak. I could walk out the front entrance of the church and walk about three or four minutes toward the south and be on the east-west runway of the airport. About another ten-minute walk and I'd be at the main airport entrance. If I traveled to the north about two hundred yards, there were the store and the post office.

Story of
Seven-One-Five-Zero-Echo

In the early summer of 2012, I came into possession of an advertisement for a Cessna 182 that was located in Ellensburg, Washington. It was a handsome airplane, and I thought perhaps it would replace the disaster of Two-Four-Niner-Niner-Golf. There had never been any indication we would ever recover any of the judgment that Don Lojek had worked so hard to win. I had been in Togiak now for over three years and greatly desired to have a set of wings. (59)

So I contacted the owner in Ellensburg, and after obtaining a list of the planes specifications, general conditions, and hours accumulated on the engine, airframe, and the prop, I made arrangements to fly down and take a look at it.

The owner met me at the Seattle airport, and we drove to his home where he kept it stored in his own hanger. In the process of dealing with the legal problems connected with Two-Four-Nine-Niner-Golf, I had become acquainted with an A&P who had his own operation at the Kelso, Washington, airport. I wanted a third party to check it out for me and to install a safety factor on the seat tracks that the manufacturer had agreed to pay to have done. The owner offered to go with me to have this accomplished and have the third party pass judgment on the general condition of the plane. I made an appointment, and the next day we went to Kelso, had the work done, and the third-party inspection made. Then we returned to Ellensburg.

I purchased the plane, and the owner asked if I was going to take it to Alaska. When I told him that was the plan, he stated that he had flown this plane at least ten times to and from Anchorage and volunteered to go with me if I would buy him a seat on a commercial flight back to Seattle. Wow! What an offer. I had some concerns, having never flown in Canada and knowing that their laws and flight rules were somewhat different than here in the USA.

He needed a few days to get his plans adjusted, so I took the plane and went to Garden Valley, had a nice visit with Carolyn, then into Deadwood and had a nice visit with Dawn and Tom. Then I went back to Ellensburg.

We left Ellensburg early in the morning making three fuel stops through British Columbia, then the fourth at White Horse, Yukon. It was about eight in the evening, and we decided to get a hotel room and then leave early in the morning. We taxied to the fuel port, and I got on the ladder and topped off both tanks. We then tied the aircraft down and went to bed. In the morning, I made a walk-around and did the pre-flight, then we were off again. It was a little over two hours to the port of entry back into the US at Northway, Alaska. There was no fuel available at the port of entry. We had four hours of fuel when we left White Horse and only had less than an hour to Glennallen, which would still leave us with an hour's reserve. I had put twenty gallons in cans in the storage compartment in case of emergency, but Kent, the former owner, and I agreed we need not get into that with the expected hour reserve.

We were about thirty minutes into our flight when the engine quit. We were over a solid wilderness of mountains and trees and were at about seven thousand feet Mean Sea Level (MSL). The well-traveled highway, the Tok Cutoff, was about twenty miles to our west, so we headed in that direction.

We almost made it. We came down in the forest, tearing the wings off, breaking out the windshield, and completely destroying the plane. We were unable to get either door open, so we had to crawl out through the windshield. (82) Kent had a sore leg that later turned out to be a hairline fracture, but he was able to walk without trouble. I had a small cut from broken glass from the windshield above my eye. After getting out, we walked thirty feet to the Tok Cutoff highway, and a vehicle stopped. I asked Kent to go with the people and report the accident to the authorities.

I would stay by, unload all the luggage, and stay with the plane. He could arrange for a vehicle to come and pick us up along with the luggage.

Right on the highway was the 65-mile marker. The state trooper in charge of the Glennallen office came about two hours later and took us with about half our luggage. He radioed back and had another vehicle come to get the rest of the luggage. As we were riding back, and the officer was in contact with the other vehicle, I asked him to ask the man if he would take the time to get the keys out of the ignition so someone would not steal the airplane. I told him I had forgotten them. He did, and they are still in my possession.

The National Transportation Safety Board (NTSB) investigates all aircraft accidents. I supplied them with all the flight records including each of the refueling stops that showed the hours in flight and the amount of fuel taken to top both tanks. They went to White Horse in the Yukon in the hopes that security cameras would have been placed where the plane was tied down. The airport did have some security cameras, but none at the location of the tie-down. The result of the investigation was that no evidence could be uncovered that would indicate that someone had stolen fuel. But there was no doubt but that is what happened, and this conclusion was shared with Kent, the previous owner, and myself.

How can I bring this story to a conclusion without calling to the attention of the reader the very obvious evidence that God has indeed been the major part of this old man's life? He is there, and I can't help but believe that He has kept me going over and over again, year after year for a reason. God has a purpose in our lives, and please, my children and grandchildren, and anyone else who reads this record, consider that He also has a purpose for each of you. Don't pass up this invitation to respond to His invitation to you

Togiak is a village of about 850 souls, 80 percent of which are native Yupik. It is my understanding that the natives here prefer to be referred to by that designation as opposed to the term Eskimo. There might be ten miles of roads in Togiak, but of course, they don't go anywhere. The only access from the outside world to the village, and for that matter to all of the villages in Western Alaska is by air, ocean-going barge, or after the winter becomes very cold and the rivers are frozen, by snowmobile to nearby villages. All of the supplies, equipment, and fuel are delivered by air, or in the summer, by barge. Heating oil is used extensively for home heating, and the electrical power is generated by large diesel engines and is delivered in large barges during the months when the water is free from ice.

The sea produces millions of pounds of fish during the summer season. There is one fish-processing factory across the bay from Togiak. The last two years I was there, a receiving station was set up where they would freeze large containers of fish, haul them to the airport, and load them by forklifts onto large C130 planes. They would then be delivered to processing centers near Anchorage. The second year that I was in Togiak, I arranged for the gift of a van to the church. I drove it from Boise, Idaho, to Anchorage. It was delivered to us by a C130. The arrangements had been made by Joe Chythlook, and there was no charge. To have vehicles shipped by barge, the cost is $2,500.

When I arrived in Togiak in the fall of 2008, the old church was standing between the new church and the street. The old parsonage was beside it, and together completely blocked the view of the new church. So when spring began to show a little life, I began to show more than a little life myself and tackled the job of changing the landscape. (83, 84, 85, 87) The old church had been a school in a distant village that completely shut down, and all the villagers moved away. I believe this action took place in the 1930s, and somehow, though no one could give me the details, the building was moved on a barge to Togiak. It had been a rather nice structure and had served the purpose well. But now was the time for it to step aside. It had a bell on it, and with more than a little effort, I devised a way to let it down by the use of some rope and dragged it into the new church and put it under the stairs. I believe it remains there to this day.

Everything about my experience connected with the four years I spent as a volunteer in Togiak has left an indelible mark on my life. I will be forever grateful for the decision I made to become involved, and for the way in which the people there took me into their community of life. The friends made there have remained so. Even now five years later I still have frequent contact by phone and mail. I would strongly encourage any person, whether young or old, male or female, to make some kind of a commitment to give something of yourselves in an effort to be a blessing to others. Alaska was a unique opportunity for me to become more of a complete person. Perhaps someplace on the equator, or a South Pacific Island, or a project in a city nearby or a neighboring state would suit you better. The important thing is to share yourself with others in some capacity.

When it was time for me to leave, Dawn and Tom came to see me home. I had arranged with Elder Crawford and his wife Coleen to be present and take the service on my last Sabbath. It was November 10, 2012. Dawn and Tom brought Faith Kenny with them from Baker City, Oregon. Faith and her husband Blaine had served as missionary teachers in Dillingham and at the school on the lake for a total of thirteen years. But that was forty or fifty years ago. Blaine had passed away a few years before my leaving, and neither he nor Faith had been back to Alaska for that many years. So this was a visit of great interest for Faith.

Dawn, Tom, and Faith had to spend several days in Dillingham because of weather. But Pastor Downs flew them up to the camp and school on the lake, so that was a renewal experience for Faith. They, along with the pastor, the Crawfords, and many others were present on the tenth as I said farewell to my very dear friends there in Togiak. Ken and Coleen presented me with a hand carved whale made from walrus tusk. We left Togiak after the service on the afternoon of November the tenth in the several airplanes that were required to carry all the visitors back to Dillingham. Then my part of the group took a commercial flight on to Anchorage.

Dawn, Tom, Faith, and I spent several days visiting points of interest along the Kenai Peninsula in an auto loaned to us by the conference. We also drove up to Palmer and visited with my friends, the Kent Sandviks, who remembered Faith from those many years before.

Then, back home to the Lower 48. I stayed with Dawn and Tom for a time, then rented a home a couple of miles away, well into the country on the large and friendly ranch of Harrell's Hereford Ranch. That became my home for the next year and a half. From there I worked diligently on the abortion issue as it affects the Christian Church.

Then there returned an urge to get back into mission work. About that time Ken Crawford asked me to return to Alaska. It sounded interesting to me, but my family strove hard to discourage my making such a move again so far from them. David Prest, president of the Idaho Conference, asked me to move into the parsonage in John Day, Oregon, and serve as volunteer pastor for the John Day, Dayville, and Long Creek churches. Another challenge of huge proportions. This, of course, would enable me to be closer to family, and that was important now that I was in my mid-eighties.

Though I entered this new responsibility with much trepidation, it seemed evident that God's hand was in it. The people in all three churches accepted me as a brother, and lasting friendships have developed. As time progressed, it became evident that my age was becoming a factor. I lost all the hearing in my right ear, and the hearing in my left ear was not more than 50 percent of what it should be. So, after nearly two years, I notified the conference that I felt it best that I resign. David Prest asked me not to so notify the churches until I had given at least thirty days in prayer and thought. He stated that he did not want me to make the move unless so directed by God. I agreed and did consider his counsel. However, it did remain evident that I should proceed with my decision. So I set the date of my departure to be January 1, 2016.

> *Though I entered this new responsibility with much trepidation, it seemed evident that God's hand was in it. The people in all three churches accepted me as a brother, and lasting friendships have developed.*

Dawn wanted me to relocate in or near Baker City again, but the Morris family, members of the Long Creek Church, asked that I consider moving into one of their ranch houses at Ritter. After a great deal more prayer and discussion with Dawn and Tom, I decided to make the move to Ritter. Dawn was disappointed but supported me in the decision. So here I am, two years later in a beautiful four-bedroom, two-bath home, situated on the top of a mountain with a view that lets me see forever.

All during this past two-year period, the Morris family have treated me far beyond anything that I deserve. It is my prayer that I can be a blessing to them and to others in some way. Within a few months, I will enter my 90th year of life, but I remain still able to function as the person I have been, of course with some obvious slowing down and other physical adjustments.

It pleased me that I was able to be actively involved in the planning and building of the new church in Long Creek. As of this writing, we hope that the church will be ready to occupy by early spring. One important issue we had to deal with was the removal of the old church. Providentially, granddaughter Becky and her husband Bryon have found a use for the church on their ranch in Spray, Oregon, and they have agreed to move it. This was an important issue because the space it occupies represents parking and access for the handicapped. It is important that this matter is cared for before the state will give us an occupancy permit. It seems so interesting how God works things out.

For some days I have thought and prayed about how best to bring this history to an effective close. Since the effort has been made as a result of several requests from my grandchildren, I would like to conclude with some well-chosen words that would encourage each of them to give serious thoughts to their eternal future. This seems to be a reasonable objective since I very much hope that we can spend the "life without end" in the company of each other.

Within a few short months, I will shed the description as an octogenarian, which has been a part of me now for just short of ten years. I must take on a new identity, perhaps best labeled as a "pre-centenarian." Pausing here to put that into perspective, I am made aware that according to the records in my possession, no other Rotthoff has ever lived to reach ninety years of age. The reason is quite clear.

None of them has ever lived to reach that antiquated station in life. Though now it is a fact that there is already one who occupies that unique status, my brother's widow, Virginia, who is still very active and in good health. Then following along in a few more months, God willing, I will follow her lead and share that coveted accomplishment.

Most of the family, brothers and sisters (except my sister Janie, who is alive and well and will hopefully continue for some additional years), parents, grandparents, uncles, aunts, nieces, nephews, cousins, etc., passed away in their 60s and 70s, with a few reaching their early 80s. One exception being my older brother Bud, who lived to his mid-eighties.

Now that the age of current life has been addressed let us get back to dealing with the future life, perhaps better understood to be eternity. This is of much greater importance even to you young grandchildren and the growing number of great-grandchildren. Do you know that in the Bible there are two different deaths identified? The first is referred to many, many times in both the Old and New Testament as a "sleep" from which we will all be awakened in what is called the resurrection. But death number two is not "sleep," it is really death from which there will be no resurrection. I will not take the time to get into the differences between the two deaths now, but to say that an understanding is very important and can be made very clear from a study of the subject in the Bible. There are some good study helps available. Give me a call. I can steer you into some excellent study material, including where it is explained in the Bible.

But this subject comes sharply into focus when we develop a desire to learn about Jesus. Who He was and who He is. What it is that He is offering, and how this offering can affect our lives now—today. Plus what it will mean tomorrow.

Seriously, my family, the greatest desire of my life is to have all of you to be with Nana and I as we are ushered into that eternal home. Remember, no more heartaches, no more parting, and no more death. So please give this your very serious consideration. It does take some effort and determination. But the results will be a forever part of your life. Why not decide now to study into this matter of salvation? I promise to give you all the help and cooperation you will need.

Respectfully, Your Pop-op

Picture Index

No doubt, most—if not all—the present generation of this family would be acquainted with the faces and the geography as displayed in this large inventory of pictures. But another generation is coming on and many of these great-grandchildren, and the generations beyond, will find it beneficial to refer to this index for the stories and details behind the pictures.

#1:   This first picture is the family of my father, Walter Rotthoff Sr., several years before he was born. As detailed in the history essay, my father was the youngest of twelve children, but this photo was made several years before his birth, most likely in the late 1890s. Seven children are pictured, so at that date four had already died, no doubt because of the many childhood diseases which were very common in the nineteenth century. Ella May, the oldest pictured, passed away some time after the picture was made. She was not part of the family when I was born.

Pictured from left to right—Back row: Gertrude and Ella May. Front row: Lenore, Fred, Adam, Emma, and Augusta. In the center are Pop and Mom, my grandparents. All but Ella May I knew well, and are identified as my uncles and aunts.

#2:   Bud and I; the location is unknown to me.

#3:   POP-OP, taken at Pop and Mom's home.

#4:   Mom, Pop, our mother, Bud, and I.

#5:   Our mother holding Bud.

#6:   Nana is the girl in the background on the diving board. Picture taken at the West Pennsylvania Junior Camp in 1948.

#7:   This picture was also taken at the West Pennsylvania Junior Camp in 1948. That is POP-OP with some of the boys. It was there Nana and I met and our courtship began soon after.

#8:   Nana and I at the family home in Wattsburg. Our courtship was getting well underway. The airplane pictured was my Aeronca Champion.

#9:   My Father before he and Mother were married.

#10:   Brothers Bud and Teddy standing, POP-OP with his dog.

#11:   Sister Janie on the calf with POP-OP standing and Ted to my left.

#12:   Nana in the year 1975. The fulfillment of her long desire to become a big-sea fisherwoman and what a success it was! Her haul was a ten-foot six-inch Sailfish and a Mia-Mia, which was a high point in her life at Acapulco.

#13:   Nana with her friend, Mary Penrod, at Junior Camp 1948. Our courtship was about to begin.

#14:   Pictured from the left—Bill Stevens, church school teacher, POP-OP, then Bud Krause, Virginia's brother who went into the ministry. The three of us conducted a short series of evangelistic meetings in Wattsburg, sometime in the early 1950s. Both Bud Krause and Bill have passed away at this writing.

#15:   My brother Bud and Virginia (well known as Sweetie) at their wedding, 1947.

#16: The home my parents built and the home where I was born, on the Hill, in Aspinwall, Pennsylvania.

#17: Still a young, single fellow. Having been discharged from the army airborne where I had been up in an airplane, perhaps thirty or forty times, but never landed in one. I purchased this Aeronica Champion for $300 and hired an instructor to teach me to fly it for $3 an hour. I kept it next to our home and flew it out of the farm field.

#18: Pictured from the left—brother Bud, Sweetie, Grandmother Vollberg, Mother, brother Teddy, and kneeling is our sister Janie with her cat and my dog, Duke.

#19: Nana, son Danny the second, and POP-OP. This had to be spring 1951.

#20: Mother, POP-OP, Danny the second, and Nana. At the family farm home.

#21: Nana, Danny the second, and POP-OP. Taken in front of the farm home that we had purchased soon after being married in 1950.

#22: Pictured from the left—Dawn and POP-OP holding Becky with Tom behind, Nana, Peggy holding Brandy, Danny the second. In the background, Arthur, Carolyn, Sandy, and Rhonda.

#23: POP-OP with Sandy, sound asleep.

#24: Dan the second, taken at Bud and Sweetie's home.

#25: Dawn, taken at Bud and Sweetie's home.

#26: Dan the second, growing up.

#27: Dawn, again at Bud and Sweetie's home.

#28: The Lowville School. Helen Craig (who is Tom Sanford's sister), Carolyn standing next to her, the two all the way to our left are Kathy Brumagin and behind her, Marylyn Reed. I am unable to remember the names of the others.

#29: Four generations. Pictured from the front—Dan the second, Grandmother Vollberg, Mother, and POP-OP.

#30: Our dairy barn with the new milk house under construction.

#31: Charlie Lord, our hired man for a couple of years, Carolyn and Danny in the foreground, and Nana. We were taking Charlie into Ohio to visit some of his family and having a picnic along the way.

#32: Carolyn in her swimming gear.

#33: Nana and I at the spike camp on Sixteen-to-One Creek, about 1965.

#34: April 12, 1951. Dan the second arrives at the Stem Memorial Hospital, Union City, Pennsylvania.

#35: June 14, 1954. Princess Dawn arrives at the Stem Memorial Hospital, Union City, Pennsylvania.

#36: Danny, Dawn, and Nana at Atlantic City, New Jersey, when it was a great family vacation spot, before they turned it into a gambling resort.

#37: Nana, Danny, and POP-OP ready for church; we are on the front lawn at the farm.

#38: The beloved Tri-Pacer. November-Niner-Seven-One-One-Delta at the Corry, Pennsylvania airport.

#39: POP-OP and Dawn at the Deadwood Outfitters Lodge.

#40: This was probably taken in the spring of 1952, with our home and dairy barn in the back ground. Those were good days with wonderful memories.

#41: The family. Taken at Bud and Sweetie's home.

#42: Danny the second, always ready to pose for a picture.

#43: A sleigh ride with our team of Shire mares. Project Patch enjoying a Garden Valley winter day.

#44: Carolyn with Binky the calf and Rebel the dog. Can't remember if the goat had a name. Taken on the front lawn. This has to be a classic.

#45: Mother and I. Mother was visiting us at our home in Valley Springs, California. This was shortly before we purchased the ranch in Garden Valley, Idaho.

#46: Nana's Sailfish displayed at our home in Garden Valley along with pictures of the trip.

#47: Nana's Mother, Cora Bair.

#48: POP-OP while serving in the occupation of Japan. About 1947.

#49: Nana and the farm dog, Suzie.

#50: Dawn doing a "cheese-cake" at the pond on the farm.

#51:   The Lowville Church. Nana and I were charter members and we gifted the pews and the chancel furniture. This was sometime around the mid-1950s.

#52:   This was our church furniture plant in Corry, Pennsylvania.

#53:   Nana at the North Pole, New York State.

#54:   This picture was taken at the Deadwood Camp. I had packed some United States Forest Service dignitaries on an inspection journey through the forest. It included the Region Ranger from Ogden, Utah, the Boise National Forest Supervisor, a couple of District Rangers, as well as a number of Lieutenants. I muscled myself into the picture also.

#55:   The Garden Valley Ranch headquarters. The home Nana and I built on the left—then the hip roofed equipment building. The old barn that we rebuilt. It was over 120 years old.

#56:   They are Nana, Karen, Sandy, Debbie, Sarah, Nicole, Amanda, Dawn, then Brandi holding Rowan.

#57:   Sister Janie and brother-in-law Floyd.

#58:   Nana and I at the Deadwood Camp.

#59:   Cessna 182, Seven-One-Five-Zero-Echo that I purchased in Ellensburg, Washington, shortly before leaving for Alaska. After spending the night in Whitehorse, Yukon Territories, where, during the night, someone stole fuel, resulting in its crashing into heavy timber some sixty miles north of Glennallen, Alaska. The plane was completely destroyed, but my passenger and I were able to walk away with only minor injuries. More evidence that God has been leading in this old man's life.

#60: Here is Cessna 182, Two-Four-Niner-Niner-Golf. The plan was to take this with me to Alaska. Here I am visiting Erin and family at Rexburg, Idaho, and wishing me well is my great-grandson Tommy.

#61: Overlooking the South Fork of the Payette River through the window wall of our home in Garden Valley, Idaho.

#62: Daughter Dawn and I at the memorial we made for Nana. The plaque reads her birth date and date of death, and the statement "NEAR THIS SPOT MARGIE REST IN SLEEP UNTIL JESUS COMES TO TAKE HER HOME." To get to this site it takes a two-hour horseback ride over a steep mountain trail.

#63: The dedication ceremony of Project Patch on the South Fork of the Payette River, Garden Valley, Idaho.

#64: Part of Project Patch's operation at Garden Valley. On the left is the boys' dorm, the dining room, kitchen, and some offices are in the center, and to the right is the girls' dorm.

#65: Nana and POP-OP.

#66: Nana and POP-OP at our home in California.

#67: Arthur and Carolyn.

#68: Son Danny getting his first haircut.

#69: On the Oregon Trail. Nana in the covered wagon pulled by our team of Shire mares and my saddle horse, Shiloh, tied to the back.

#70:   Granddaughter Sarah and great-granddaughter Haylee Rae.

#71:   Great-grandchildren Imriel and Rhalpsody.

#72:   Great-granddaughter Alessandra Rae.

#73:   Debbie and POP-OP.

#74:   POP-OP and great granddaughter Briana.

#75:   Great-granddaughter Briana.

#76:   Great-grandson Jake.

#77:   Granddaughter Nicole.

#78:   Brother Bud, Sister Janie, POP-OP.

#79:   POP-OP and Killer.

#80:   TJ and POP-OP walking away from the old barn at Deadwood.

#81:   Two great-granddaughters, Haylee and Alessandra.

#82:   Seven-One-Five-Zero-Echo after the engine ran out of fuel.

#83:   The old church in Togiak, Alaska, soon to be torn down. The new church is behind it.

#84:   Baptismal class in Togiak.

#85:   Martha Fox and Pastor Wendell Downs.

#86: Maco and Tassie transporting newlyweds at Project Patch.

#87: Martha Fox and newly adopted baby girl. My Togiak visit 2016.

#88: Nana and the Aeroncia. We were not yet married.

#89: Retha Eldridge and her two children. She and her husband, Paul, and the children spent all the war years in a Japanese concentration camp in the Philippines. She gave me a copy of her book, *Bombs and Blessings*, while I was at the mission in Japan, 1948.

#90: POP-OP and Elder B.P. Hoffman. This missionary took me under his wing and gave me a tour of many areas in and around Tokyo. Here in front of a giant Buddha.

#91: My sister Janie and Floyd's wedding at the Erie, Pennsylvania, church.

#92: POP-OP walking Carmela down the aisle to give her away.

#93: The wedding day and the Sanitarium Chapel, Tacoma Park, Maryland.

#94: Carolyn and Arthur's wedding day. Erie SDA Church.

#95: Brother Bud and POP-OP.

#96: On our wedding day. March 12, 1950.

#97: This was perhaps taken thirty-five years later—somewhere around the mid-1980s.

#98:   This was taken around the time of the gift of the ranch to Project Patch. 1989–1990.

#99:   One of my very most favorite pictures, at the ranch in Garden Valley.

#100:   Back on the farm in Pennsylvania. 1951.

#101:   After a couple days of threshing with the old grain separator.

#102:   POP-OP, Nana, and Nana's youngest brother Glenn in front of the farm home, sometime around the mid-fifties.

#103:   Mert and Annette Beam, Dawn, and POP-OP at Nana's burial site high on a ridge, two hours on horseback from the Deadwood base camp. There we had fastened into a granite rock a plaque indicating that here she would rest until Jesus came to take her home. I try to make the journey into the site every year.

#104:   Becky and her colt.

#105:   Erin, dressed in early American garb, and her mount on a memorable trip on the Oregon Trail.

#106:   Erin and Joe's marriage at the Baker City, Oregon, SDA Church.

#107:   Nana, her first organ in our home in Montrose, California.

#108:   Sweetie, Bud, Dawn, and Nana at Three Rivers, California.

#109:   Nana and her horse Susie, Angeles National Forest, California.

Pictures

#1

#2

#3

#4

#5

#6

#7

#8

#9

#10

#11

#12

#13

#14

#15

#16

#17

#18

#19

#20

#21

#22

#23

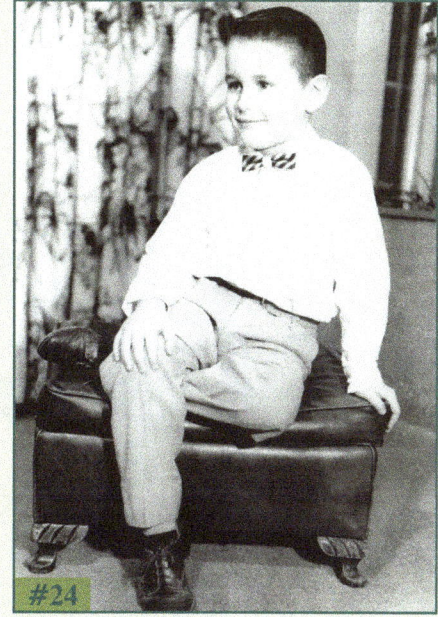

#24

#25

#26

#27

#28

#29

#30

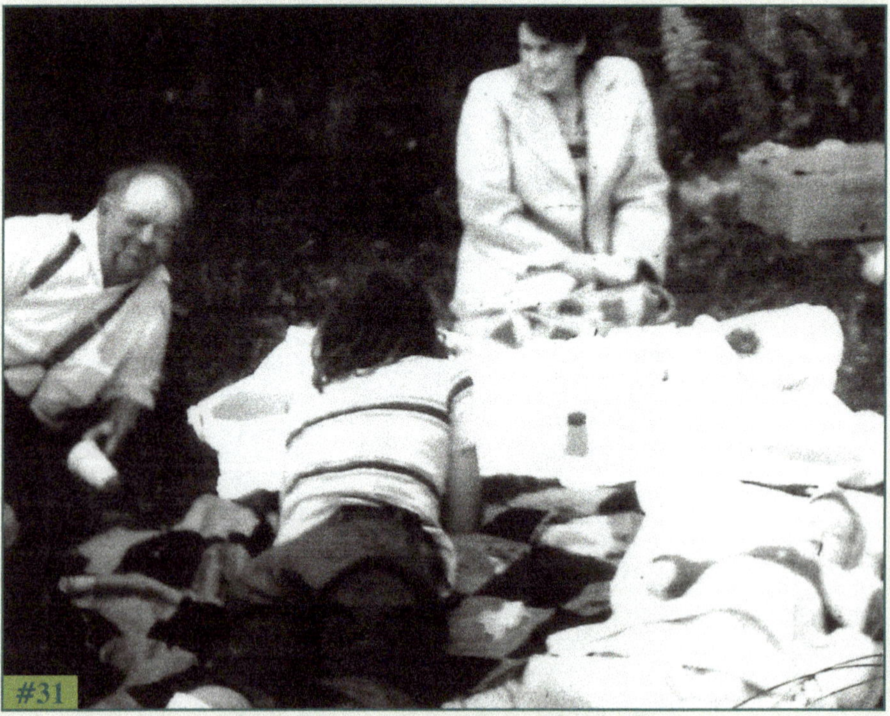

#31

#32

#33

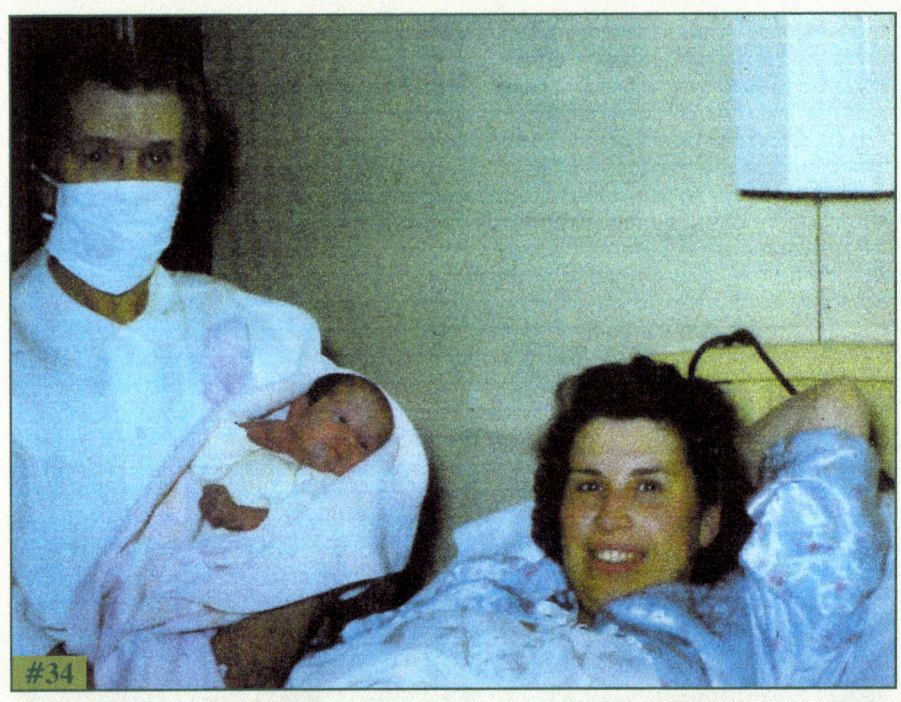

#34

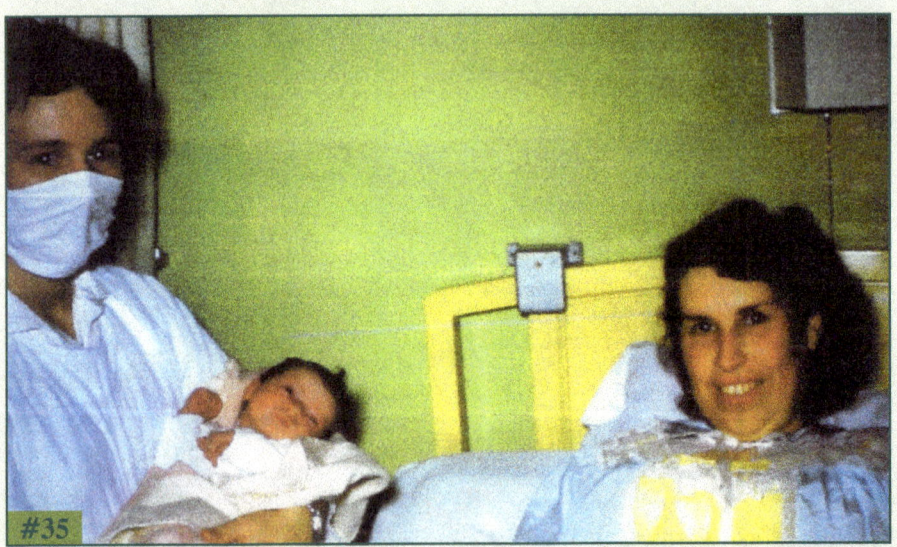

#35

#36

#37

#38

#39

#40

#41

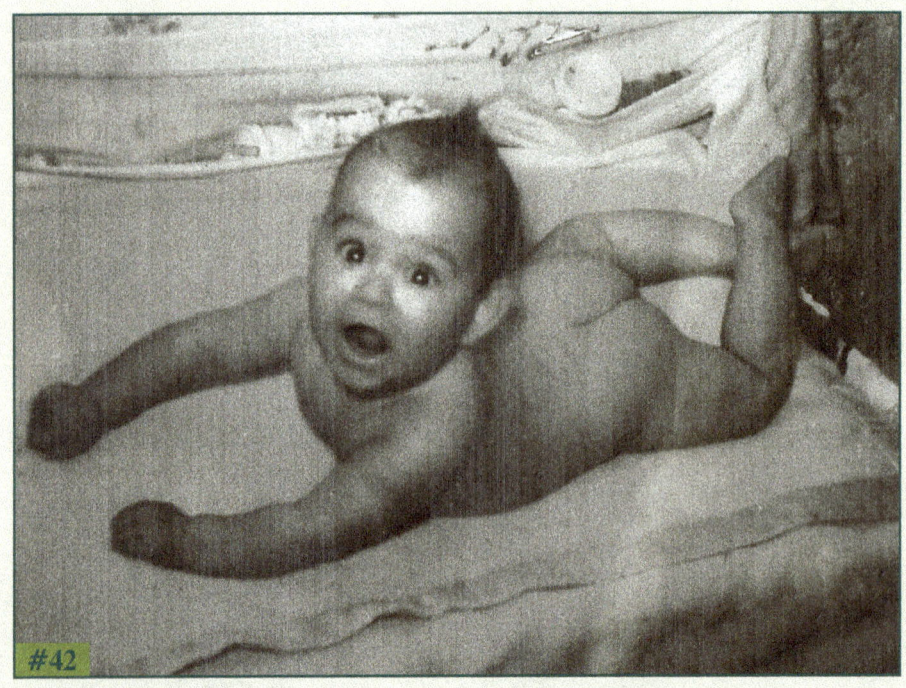

#42

#43

#44

#45

#46

#47

#48

#49

#50

#51

#52

#53

#54

#55

#56

#57

#58

#59

#60

#61

#62

#63

#64

#65

#66

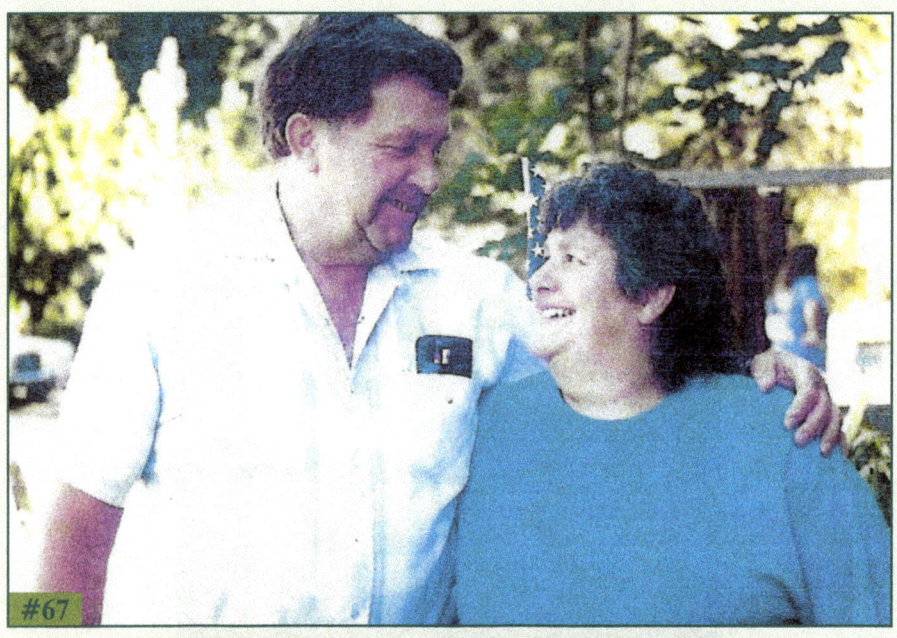

#67

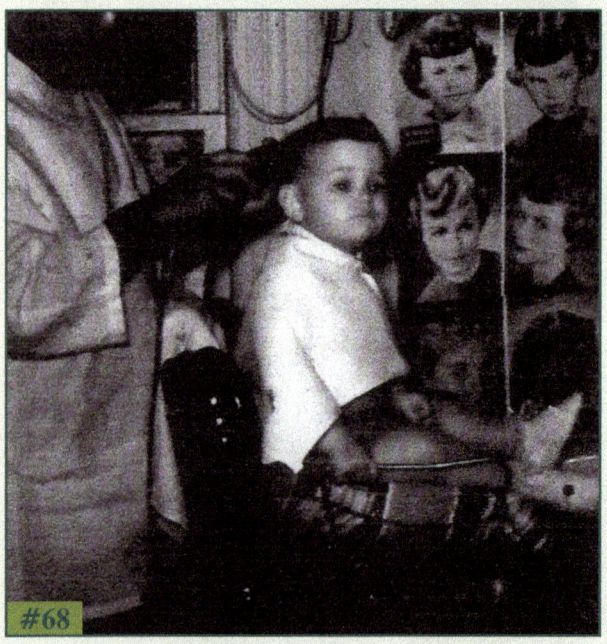

#68

#69

#70

#71

#72

#73

#74

#75

#76

#77

#78

#79

#80

#81

#82

#83

#84

#85

#86

#87

#88

#89

#90

#91

#92

#93

#94

#95

#96

#97

#98

#99

#100

#101

#102

#103

#104

#105

#106

#107

#108

#109

#110

#111

#112

#113

#114

#115

#116

TEACH Services, Inc.
P U B L I S H I N G
www.TEACHServices.com • (800) 367-1844

We invite you to view the complete
selection of titles we publish at:
www.TEACHServices.com

We encourage you to write us
with your thoughts about this,
or any other book we publish at:
info@TEACHServices.com

TEACH Services' titles may be purchased in
bulk quantities for educational, fund-raising,
business, or promotional use.
bulksales@TEACHServices.com

Finally, if you are interested in seeing
your own book in print, please contact us at:
publishing@TEACHServices.com

We are happy to review your manuscript at no charge.

CPSIA information can be obtained
at www.ICGtesting.com
Printed in the USA
BVHW010304080319
542042BV00013B/696/P